The Happy Me Project

T0029606

The Happy Me Project

The no-nonsense guide to self-development

Holly Matthews

GREEN TREE

LONDON · OXFORD · NEW YORK · NEW DELHI · SYDNEY

GREEN TREE
Bloomsbury Publishing Plc
50 Bedford Square, London, WC1B 3DP, UK
29 Earlsfort Terrace, Dublin 2, Ireland

BLOOMSBURY, GREEN TREE and the Green Tree logo are trademarks
of Bloomsbury Publishing Plc

First published in Great Britain 2022

A catalogue record for this book is available from the British Library

Library of Congress Cataloguing-in-Publication data has been applied for

ISBN: TPB: 978-1-4729-8661-0; eBook: 978-1-4729-8659-7; ePDF: 978-1-4729-8658-0

2 4 6 8 10 9 7 5 3 1

Typeset by Deanta Global Publishing Services, Chennai, India
Printed and bound in Great Britain by CPI Group (UK) Ltd, Croydon CRO 4YY

MIX
Paper from
responsible sources
FSC® C171272

To find out more about our authors and books visit www.bloomsbury.com
and sign up for our newsletters

For Brooke and Texas, my incredible daughters who inspire me and impress me every single day. I love you girls, you're awesome in ways you can't even comprehend!

Dedicated to Ross, I miss you pal.

Contents

Introduction

At 12 years old I was a closet meditator, finding my own way to deal with my issues. I found some classical music on a cassette at home in a drawer and began listening to it regularly, secretly turning it on, then closing my eyes and calmly breathing in and out. I didn't know what I was doing, it was guesswork at this point, but these early attempts at meditation seemed to help.

It was 1998 and I was kitted out in Adidas tracksuit bottoms and Nike Air Max trainers. I had scrunchies in my high ponytail, which was scraped back off my head and sticky with hairspray. I had not long been cast in an award-winning kids TV show called *Byker Grove* – a cult programme that at its height was averaging 5 million viewers per episode. I was struggling to find the balance between suddenly spending half my time filming and the rest of my time going to a 'normal' school in working-class Newcastle upon Tyne.

Self-help, mental health and meditating were definitely not things my friends were talking about and, without access to the internet, I was very much making it up as I went along. Thankfully for me, the world has moved on since then and I am now firmly out of the 'meditating closet' and fully immersed in finding tangible ways to help myself and others to feel good. In fact, I've made it my profession, as a life coach, neuro-linguistic programming (NLP) practitioner and hypnotherapist.

The self-help space can sometimes feel a little 'woo woo' and preachy, with some of my more spiritual counterparts whooping, hollering and talking about God. There isn't, of course, anything wrong with this if it feels good to you, but if you're anything like me then the flowery and over-the-top type of personal development just doesn't really appeal. That's where this book comes in.

In it, I share my own journey, what I have learned along the way, and some tips, tricks, tools and ponderings so that you can navigate yourself through your own hectic and challenging lives and still enjoy yourself along the way. Some of these challenges will be huge life events, such as deaths and illness, and others will be the mundane struggles we all face, such as the never-ending conveyor belt of dishes and washing that are part of everyday living. Or perhaps you are someone who compares yourself to strangers on social media and suffers from self-esteem issues as a consequence. All of this can impact how happy we feel. Whatever you're facing, this book can help.

I will be straight talking and sometimes brutally real with you and I invite you to embrace this approach because sometimes we need tough love. Just know that it's all done with the best of intentions and a genuine desire to help you create a life that feels 'more happy and less crappy'. I've written this book to help you gain some insight and guide you through some of the challenges that you might face.

As many of us have the attention span of gnats due to our excessive, and often unhealthy, addiction to social media and smartphones (I'm totally guilty of this, too, don't worry), I have structured this book to be as user-friendly as possible. It consists of 60 short, sharp chapters with a list of actionable steps you can take at the end of each. You are not expected to read in a linear fashion from cover to cover. This is *your* book and it should be read in a way that feels right to you. Pick it up, put it down, flick through it, get the highlighter pens out and mark your favourite bits, read it on the toilet, take a ton of photos and share them on your Instagram page (make sure you tag me @iamhollymatthews, so I can thank you and watch your progress). Do whatever feels right.

If you'd like to delve a bit deeper into any of the points or studies I've mentioned in this book, then I've popped all the references on my website: www.iamhollymatthews.com/references/. I wanted to veer away from making this a heavy academic text, so we could keep things as simple as possible (but they're all there for you if you want to know more).

Why me?

I don't profess to be the oracle of anything. I'm not some self-development 'guru' who takes myself seriously and expects everyone else to. I'm going to tell you from the very outset that I am flawed AF.

Some days I cry, some days I doubt myself. Some days I'm consumed by the guilt of being a mum of two daughters and worry that I'm messing them up in a way that they will possibly be discussing with a therapist in the future.

I am far from perfect. I tell you this because none of us are perfect and I want us to be on the same level here, human to human.

What I *do* bring to the table, however, is 20-plus years of trying to make sense of who I am and the benefit of having delved into a lot of the self-development stuff that's out there in the world. As mentioned already, I'm also a professional life coach, NLP practitioner (sounds fancy, right?) and hypnotherapist, and someone who has always been obsessed with how our minds work.

Growing up wanting to be an actress meant I was extremely driven and often felt very different to my friends and peers. I know that sounds egocentric, but I just often felt like I was playing a game, pretending to understand their world and acting out the part accordingly (many years later I was diagnosed with ADHD, and so perhaps this had an influence on some of these feelings).

I became a professional actress very young and believe me when I say that being on TV while going to a normal school made me a target. I spent half of my time filming and half of my time at school and would often sneak home after filming (telling the driver who was meant to drop me off at the school gates that I had forgotten my PE kit or homework), so that I didn't have to face being whispered about or picked on for being 'the girl off the telly'.

I masked my insecurities well with a full face of terribly applied make-up (no YouTube tutorials for us 90s' kids) and fake confidence. I was in the 'popular' group at school, but I was totally and utterly lost.

I spent my time at home listening to Alanis Morissette's *Jagged Little Pill* album and hypnosis CDs I'd borrowed from the local library. Outside my house, I hung around the streets with my friends, getting drunk on cheap wine and listening to dance music.

At the age of 18, after seven years on children's TV, I signed to a major record label as a solo singer and felt like things were really moving forwards for me. I suddenly found myself touring round the UK, appearing on TV shows and radio stations, and seeing myself on MTV. I was around people who bolstered my ego and promised the earth.

I was travelling between London and Newcastle, and appearing in magazines such as *Elle Girl*. I'd feature in articles entitled 'A week in the life of...' and have my photo taken at fake events, buying flowers for my non-existent London apartment, and generally act the part of a celebrity.

It's weird looking back on that time because in reality I was on my own a lot. Staying in hotels alone, missing my family and really having no clue what I wanted from life or whether I was even enjoying my current reality.

Then, in 2004, the music industry started really changing. People weren't buying physical CDs any more and my single got caught up in this shift. One Sunday night, during the weekly singles charts, it trundled in at number 32 out of 40 on the Radio 1 chart show. The next morning, I received a call from a record label executive to say, 'Thanks for working with us, good luck and good bye.'

I went from celebrity parties, fancy hotels and the prospect of potentially being friends with J.Lo (OK, no one had told me that would happen, but I was kinda hoping it'd be the case!) to working in a coffee shop, quietly serving customers and pondering my next steps.

It was a major wake-up call and it made me realise, for probably the first time, that things don't always go to plan; a lesson that would ultimately serve me well in the coming years.

Alongside working in the cafe, I had acquired a talent agent and was travelling back and forth to London for auditions. I began booking jobs and appeared on many popular shows in the UK, but for every job I booked there were 10 unsuccessful auditions where I didn't get the part. The process of auditioning and failing time and time again made me feel crap about myself and I had to work hard to get over this – a process that over time made me extremely resilient.

During this period, I also met my husband Ross, an eccentric man who had his own business and spoke his mind (often to his detriment). It was a meeting of two lone wolves who managed to connect enough to want to live together and get married. When I found out I was pregnant, Ross's calm reaction was simply to smile and say 'good age' and at 26 we began a new stage in our relationship.

In 2011, I became a mum for the first time, to my daughter Brooke. The little monkey turned up six weeks early after a bout of pre-eclampsia and Ross and I spent the first few weeks of her life in the Special Care Baby Unit, with our very tiny, fragile baby. Brooke made it home, but then at just three months old she was rushed back into hospital with meningitis. Happily, after a scary week in hospital, this tough little baby could return home again.

In 2013, I became a mum for the second time, to my daughter Texas. This pregnancy was a difficult one after the whole pre-eclampsia lark and I was also diagnosed with something called antiphospholipid syndrome (apparently I have 'sticky' blood), so I had to inject blood thinners into my pregnant stomach, which was pretty horrible.

The thing with all of these challenges, though, was that I just dealt with them as they came, without feeling sorry for myself or dwelling on them. They all seemed like things that just happened. I guess it's only in retrospect that we recognise the enormity of what we have been through.

Then, in 2014, life got really real, really quickly.

My husband Ross had been experiencing some really dark, depressive moods, which we'd just put down to the fast-paced change of being a new parent. However, following some severe headaches and lots of back-and-forth to the doctors and hospital, Ross was given the news everyone dreads.

Brain cancer.

The bad kind.

The kind where you know, no matter what happens, that things are about to get tough and your life will change forever.

I was terrified.

I can vividly remember coming home from the hospital for the first time on my own since his diagnosis. I sat on the kitchen floor and sobbed. Really, really sobbed. The kind of sobbing that you think will never stop. Ugly sobbing. And then I can remember the moment my mindset shifted.

Because in that moment of despair, I realised that if I wanted myself and my family to get through this time in our lives then it was down to me; no one else was going to save me and this was happening whether we wanted it to or not.

And I decided to do whatever it took to be happy, regardless of crappy cancer.

In July 2017, after three and a half years of cancer and everything that this involves – the chemo, the radiotherapy, the brain surgeries, a whole heap of appointments, seizures and endless tablets – my beautiful, quirky and hilarious husband died.

Just writing that gave me the feeling I have often experienced over the past few years, the same disbelief: 'What on earth? How is he dead?'

You see, many of us really can't imagine people dying unless they're old and in their beds, right? I know, logically, we get it, but it's only ever an abstract concept until it's someone *you* love.

After Ross died, my life *did* change forever. *I* changed forever.

Now you could read that sentence and think I mean it in a negative way, but truly I don't. I mean my life changed, for both good and bad and a little in between.

The biggest change for me was recognising that I haven't got a clue about anything. How can I possibly understand the world? The world I knew, the one that made sense – *that* world most definitely had my husband alive in it. This new world, without him, meant I had to rethink everything.

The past few years have been a journey of much deeper self-discovery. I've let go of judgement, lived more vulnerably and had to question what really matters to me. I've lived with true bravery and I have felt more empathy for others than I thought possible.

All of this life experience I have just skimmed over is why this book has come to fruition. I'm on a mission: no BS, no fluff, I'm going to share with you what I've learned and I'm keeping it simple. Because one major thing to come out of all this chaos is my absolute desire to help people to create and live a life they love. Time is so short and I want you to be happy.

Delve into this book with an open mind, share it with your cynical friend and laugh through the madness that is our daily lives. I hope it lets you see that you're not alone and that those wild thoughts and daily struggles are universal.

Make sure you chat to me on social media about your light-bulb moments because I adore hearing about how you have come through your challenges and what you've tried out (the weirder the better). I want to know what in this book has helped. You can find me at @iamhollymatthews on Instagram and Facebook and @hollymatthews on Twitter.

You've got this. Even when you really don't feel like 'you've got this', you do. Take this book and create a life that is unbreakable and packed with joy.

Holly x

#1

How the brain works

I love learning about the brain. I find it fascinating. And the more I learn, the more I realise our brains are working perfectly – that is, they function and respond according to what we give them access to.

As this is the beginning of the book (even if some of you have started in the middle), I feel it's appropriate to begin by sharing the science behind what is going on in that head of yours.

We have around 60,000 thoughts per day (although if you're an overthinker, like me, I'm fairly sure we have that many just while drinking a cup of coffee!), and our brains take in around 4 billion bits of data per second. That is *a lot* of information.

However, neurotypical people are usually not consciously aware of all of this information. This is because there is a collection of nerve cells in the brain stem called the reticular activating system – or RAS for short. The RAS is like the little doorman of the conscious mind and it decides what it will and won't let through. It's essentially the brain's filtering system.

So what does it let in? There are certain things that always get past the RAS (again, if you're neurotypical), for example: if you're in danger, if a loved one's in danger or if someone calls out your name. In these cases, your RAS will open the door and bring this information to the forefront of your mind super quickly, so your focus can be on it.

In general, the brain has a strong confirmation bias, which simply means that we as humans like to be right (and don't we know it!). So, as it's sifting through the data, it will be seeking out anything that matches up with what you already believe about the world, what you already believe about yourself, and what you spend lots of your time focused on.

Now this is fantastic news if you're a super-positive person who believes the world is a glorious place laced with endless possibilities, and you focus your attention on joy, abundance and love. This is not so much fun if your mind is foggy with negativity and your focus is always on the worst-case scenario.

Personally, this means that if I am in a negative headspace and every day I tell myself I'm fat, ugly and no one likes me, my brain is going to search through all the data and look for evidence to back this theory up, bringing these negative thoughts fully into my focus.

Say a friend doesn't text me back. Well, that goes straight into the 'no one likes me' pile of information. Should someone say I look 'different' today, that can be filtered into the 'I'm fat and ugly' pile. Both of these comments could be completely innocent, but while my RAS is switched firmly to 'the world is a negative place and no one likes me' I will continue to process information in this way and negativity will continue to show up for me. You can almost imagine it like the algorithms we have on social media. If I like posts about 'cleaning hacks' then I'm guaranteed to see mops, cloths and lint rollers on my feed for the next few weeks, and our RAS is the algorithm of our beliefs.

You may have heard the phrase 'what we think about, we bring about', which suggests that the more time you spend focusing on the things you don't want, the more your brain is going to bring those undesirable things into your focus. How annoying is that?

However, on the flip side, once you start focusing on the things you *do* want and love, your brain's algorithm assumes you want to see more of that … which of course you do!

In positive psychologist Sonja Lyubomirsky's book *The How of Happiness: A Practical Guide to Getting the Life You Want* (Piatkus, 2010), she surmises that 50 per cent of our happiness is based on genetics and 10 per cent on circumstances, leaving 40 per cent of our happiness in our control. Essentially, there may be a certain genetic set point that determines how positive or negative we feel naturally (and there's really not a great deal you can do about that), but there is a huge chunk of your happiness that you are in control of. That is where your focus should go.

> **'There is a huge chunk of your happiness that you are in control of and that is where your focus should go.'**

Psychologists believe that we have a negativity bias, meaning that when something negative happens we think about it far more than we would something positive. When we consider how we have evolved, this makes sense. When we were cave men and women running around in furry pants trying not to be killed or have our food stolen, we had to make quick decisions in order to stay alive.

We haven't really changed all that much since then. We still possess, and rely on, a primitive part of our brain called the amygdala (sometimes known as the 'reptilian brain'). This is quick to react and is in charge of our survival. It controls our need to feed, fight, flee and ... reproduce. To do this, it seeks out the negative, looks for the dangers lurking around every corner and is constantly on guard to keep us safe.

We therefore need the amygdala – it's very important – but we also need another part of our brain to help us decide whether we really are under attack. This part is called the frontal lobe, which is located right at the front of the brain. This controls emotional expression, problem solving, memory, language, judgement, and both our social and, ahem, sexual interests.

Now you know a little more about what's going on inside your brain, you might see that in order to feel happy, you have to put in a little graft. You have to make an effort to protect your brain and make sure that you are giving it all the tools it needs to run in a way that works for you.

If we feed our bodies junk food all day every day, we can expect to get sick, tired and physically unfit. Similarly, if we feed our mind junk all day, we can expect to feel stressed, fed-up, overwhelmed and unhappy.

It is time to protect your mind. In this book, I'm going to give you a whole heap of ways that you can do this. I suggest you take it seriously. I might deliver my message in a way that's light-hearted, but I'm serious when I say we need to train our brain and shift our filtering system to work in our favour.

How do I get my brain working for me?

1 **Don't worry about how you're feeling** right now or how you've felt in the past. TODAY we begin your journey to creating a more positive space for your brain. In this book, you're going to learn how to feed yourself a gourmet lunch of positivity.

2 **Listen to your thoughts** and think about how they might be affecting the world you see. Keep a diary for a week and begin to notice words that you use a lot as these are the ones that will eventually change how you perceive things. I then encourage you to start challenging these words and consider if they are helping or hindering you. If they help you then carry on. If they hinder you then decide what you can replace them with.

3 **Stop and look around wherever you are** and find five things that are beautiful, joyous, sweet, pretty or that make you smile. I don't care whether you're reading this on your lunch break, on the bus or on the beach – look around, find your joy. Doing this regularly is like giving your brain a healthy snack to add to the overall picture of having a healthy, happy mind. We can call these your 'joy carrots'!

#2

That old belief is holding you back

Many people aren't living the life they want. They are settling for what they think they can have, what they think they deserve and what is easily available to them. Many people drift from moment to moment, allowing life to knock them about like a shiny metal ball in a pinball machine.

They make decisions based on necessity and what they think they're supposed to do. They limit their thinking to what those around them have been able to achieve and they're very often not leading the life they want because they've never actually taken the time to consider what that is.

This type of thinking creates sentences like 'people like me don't have houses like that' or 'I can't start my own business, I'm not smart enough'. This is what we call a 'limiting belief'. A limiting belief is simply that: a belief that is limiting your life in some way. In any area of your life that you are finding difficult, you will find a load of sneaky limiting beliefs hiding under the surface in your subconscious mind.

You see, our conscious mind is good as gold. Our conscious mind is that part of us that sets goals, starts the diet, decides to create all these new and wonderful habits. However, it's our subconscious mind that is *really* running the show.

So, if in our conscious mind we are saying, 'I want to be the most successful person in my workplace, I'm going to hit that target and get the promotion' (add in your own air punch here), but lurking in the murky depths of our subconscious mind is the belief that we aren't good enough, and that no one in our family has ever made that kind of money so it's unlikely we will, then guess which wins the day? Yep! The subconscious mind.

Now, again, this is subconscious and not something you are even necessarily aware is going on. But what can happen when these negative thoughts bubble underneath is that you don't really push yourself or take action towards the things you want. Perhaps you even slip into full-blown self-sabotage, which is when you do things to destroy, damage or obstruct yourself from achieving the things you want.

This all happens because our subconscious and our conscious minds are conflicted. Let's imagine your conscious mind is looking for a loving relationship. You say it out loud, you tell your friends and you take action by joining a few dating apps and going out more. But let's also imagine that in the darkest underbelly of your subconscious mind is the belief that all people are cheats and liars. If this is the case, then you, my friend, have a conflict.

In reality, what may happen in this particular tug of war is that for a time your angelic-like conscious mind will lead the way and begin looking for the perfect partner, but because your cunning subconscious mind is still telling your brain that all people are cheats and liars, your brain will assume that you want to see more people who fit into this category. Which, of course, you don't!

Alternatively, you may find that because your subconscious thoughts are strong, after a few less-than-successful first dates, you just accept defeat and give up the quest altogether.

This does not need to happen. In order for us to live a life that fills our hearts with joy, we need to poke around in the dusty corners of our subconscious and pull these limiting beliefs to the surface, where we can deal with them.

In one of my workshops a few years back a lady raised her hand when we discussed limiting beliefs and said, 'What if your limiting belief isn't a belief at all, it's a fact?' An interesting concept, I thought, and asked her to explain further. 'Well, I want to be successful in my business, but I'm a highly sensitive person and I cry a lot. I just know that this means I'll fail because successful people don't cry at meetings.' I told her that this was a limiting belief because for every time she told herself this story there was another person crying all the way to a hugely successful business. In fact, it has been said that Steve Jobs was a crier and I'm fairly confident he did all right for himself.

Once we begin to dig out these beliefs, we can then start to change them, or at the very least be aware of them and on the look-out at times when we know they may be triggered.

When you finally work out what your subconscious has been up to, you may find it even feels a little ridiculous when you say the beliefs out loud. For example, I had lots of limiting beliefs around money. My parents didn't have a lot of money, but I started earning at the age of 11 (even though I didn't have access to it then). I discovered then that once I got money people weren't that keen on it. 'Who do you think you are?' and 'Do you have £100 for your dinner money?' were phrases I heard regularly at school. After a bit of work on my mind as an adult, I realised that I still held the belief that 'If I make money, I'll make other people feel uncomfortable.'

I still feel a little silly that this belief was (and sometimes still is) there. Noticing the absurdity of the beliefs can help shift them.

How to get rid of your limiting beliefs

1 **Think about the sticky areas of your life**, whether it's social life, relationships, work life or even how you feel about the way you look. Write down some beliefs you have about them: 'I am ugly and

no one will ever love me!', 'I'll always struggle with money' or 'I just can't make friends.'

2 **Write down facts that contradict these initial statements**. 'I just can't make friends' could be 'I once had a lovely friend in my old job, but we just lost touch.' 'Everyone thinks I'm ugly and I will never have a partner' could be 'I was given a compliment last week by my mate Priya.'

3 **Create powerful affirmation sentences** to replace the old beliefs. For example, 'Money comes easily to me', 'I love meeting new people' and 'I am a kind and loveable person.'

4 **Explore where these beliefs came from**. I guarantee the majority came from some offhand comment from someone else (you're thinking about the exact words they said right now, aren't you?), which may not have even been intentionally hurtful. Recognising where the thoughts were born can help to minimise their impact.

5 **Laugh at the crazy subconscious thoughts** – their silliness, their ridiculousness – and dampen their flames. They're just thoughts and *you* are in control, not them.

'**Never let an old story hold you back from a new life.**'

#3

Stop moaning!

The last time you picked up the phone to a friend, what was the topic of conversation? Was it your dreams, your desires, the goals you're setting for yourself and all things positive? Did you both share stories of the kindness you'd witnessed that day at work and pay thanks to your children, partner and work colleagues for being with you on this glorious journey?

Oh, it wasn't? Not even close? Well, that's not a surprise... As human beings, we spend an inordinate amount of time moaning and groaning, and the list of things we have to complain about is simply endless. The weather (too hot or too cold), the traffic, public transport, our partners and children, spam emails, the WiFi, people's loud eating, having to get up early, bad hair days, work, ironing – truly nothing is exempt as a topic of our constant griping and grumbling.

What is our problem? Why do we feel the need to spew out negative thoughts in a mindless loop of pessimism?

Well, first off, it helps us to alleviate some stress. You know the feeling – moaning lets off some steam and it feels good to blame external factors for how we feel. Getting a moment to whinge about Colin from work and how he constantly interrupts you in meetings, or having a listening ear while you spit venom about your ex-boyfriend, can simply feel nice.

Second, it's a good way to bond with people. Group complaining can connect us, especially if we agree on our chosen topic of complaint. If we all agree that Chris from accounts shouldn't eat his mackerel salad in the communal area, for example, and we moan together about it during Friday night drinks, this helps us to feel validated and part of a group.

Group complaining can also help us work through our problems. Being able to vent allows us a way to spitball ideas outside of our own heads and there can definitely be benefits to this.

Another hidden kick we receive from our moaning is the secondary gains we get. We all have that friend who perpetually puts up Facebook statuses about her weekly trials and tribulations and is then inundated with offers of support and 'Are you OK hun?'-type messages. Getting attention in return for the public complaining is a prime example of a secondary gain. Moaning = reward.

Our families and our upbringing may also be a big factor in why we are serial complainers. If you grew up in a household where the culture was to come home and lament the stresses of your day then it isn't surprising that you have grown up to be a complainer, too.

Once we start on the complain loop it forms as a habit and very quickly becomes what we do regularly. You may even have friends or family to whom you honestly wouldn't know what to talk about if you didn't have your big bag of 'all the things going wrong in my world right now' to drop into conversation.

You may well be reading this and thinking, 'OK, Holly, so what's the big deal though, you said it alleviates stress, so why can't I be left to my own devices?' And I agree, you can. Your life is completely your own and, as with everything, a little occasional moan is fine. However, when you slip into chronic and incessant moaning, it starts to have a negative impact on your mental health (and also likely on your relationships with others).

My biggest issue with moaning is that for the most part we do nothing about the actual problems and allow them to fester. We might be really wound up that we have been overlooked for the promotion for the second time when we feel we deserve it, but we never actually sit down for an honest conversation with our boss to seek feedback. Moaning can lead to inaction. It's the easier option than doing something about the issue. It's a comfy space, where you get to complain without doing the work.

Continuous moaning really does have a negative impact on our health too. When we get into our moments of unstoppable moaning, we begin to train our brain that the world is a miserable place, which causes our body to releases a stress hormone called cortisol. If cortisol is activated too much then it can increase blood pressure, weaken the immune system and even increase the risk of heart disease.

On the more trivial side, being the one who moans but is never willing to do anything differently may become draining for your friends and family. If you're dumping the same problems on them day in and day out then you may find they start to distance themselves as your negativity begins to impact them too.

Moaning doesn't solve problems, it just creates them. The more you talk about the same problems without actually taking steps to work through them or change what's going on, the more worked up about them you will become. It's essentially fuel for the fire when it comes to feeling miserable.

I want to stop moaning, but I don't know how

1 **Get curious about why you're moaning so much**. Are you tired, overworked, overwhelmed, scared? Investigate where it's coming from. Once you work out what's happening, establish whether there is something that can be done about the situation and get to it. If it's out of your control, can you find a different way to discuss the same subject?

2 **Notice your triggers**. If you know you're going to feel stressed after the morning school run and want to moan to everyone you can find, think about what you can do to get in front of those feelings and find something different to do instead of whining. Why not try declaring your joy for things out loud instead? Use the three Es: excitedly, enthusiastically and expressively. Boldly say 'I love that colour car.' 'I adore the smell of the perfume I just spritzed myself with.' 'How wonderful the sky looks today.' This technique forces you to focus on joy.

3 **Write it out**. Get the moans down on paper and when you've finished, bin them and let them go.

4 **Give yourself a moaning allowance**. You're allowed either one or two small moans a day to be used wisely, or a 10-minute moaning window during which you're allowed to enjoy wallowing in your complaints. Once the time is up, though, you have to stop.

5 **Take action!** For the real complaints, where there is a genuine issue, take steps towards resolving the situation. Stop dwelling on the issue and start empowering yourself by changing it moving forwards.

'Moaning doesn't solve problems, it just creates them.'

#4

Mix it up

Have you ever watched a hamster on its wheel? As a child, I had about 10 different hamsters over the years (and stuck with the same name three times over because I couldn't face the fact that Clarky (version 1) had in fact died). So, in my time I have watched many a hamster go round and round and round in their wheels, seemingly without tiring. When I imagine this hamster wheel now I equate it to times in my life when I haven't felt so great about where I'm headed or when I've realised I'm not going anywhere very fast at all.

A recent study found that only three out of 10 people are happy with their lives and that 69 per cent felt tired of the same old routine. 'Stuck in a rut' is a phrase that I hear a lot from some of my newest clients and I'm fairly confident we've all experienced this feeling.

When we stay in this rather lacklustre space for any period of time, we might begin to feel a bit sad, uninspired, bored or lacking in energy. The daily monotony can leave us feeling helpless. If you're reading this now and nodding along then we are about to shake things up for you!

Your life is happening *now* and, if you stay in the position you're currently in, you're going to drive yourself mad with boredom. What's more, it's completely unnecessary. As Albert Einstein is often quoted as saying, 'Insanity is doing the same thing over and over again and expecting different results'.

Now, of course, as responsible adults we have to contend with a certain amount of routine and a dollop of the mundane, and there's nothing wrong with this as it can actually help us to see where we have space to mix things up. Mixing things up doesn't have to mean a complete life overhaul (unless of course that's what you want). It can mean daily tweaks to our lives that help us to feel alive and engaged in the world around us.

Don't underestimate the power of the tweak. A little change can make all the difference, and when we do this consistently in our lives it keeps things fresh and interesting.

Just this week, after slipping into the humdrum of life for a while, I decided that I needed to do something different. I noticed that Airbnb were hosting online events, some of which were extraordinarily weird and niche. As a person who likes to try new things, I booked myself into various online sessions, including laughter therapy with a lovely couple called Cath and Tom, learning magic with Aleksandr from Estonia, and a meditation class with a Buddhist monk from Tibet. There was also 'meet the dogs of Cherynobl' and 'Sangria and secrets with drag queens'. All in all, it was a busy week!

So, how can you begin mixing things up?

It can truly be as simple as changing your house around by putting up some new pictures or treating yourself to some new bedding. It could be shaking up your own wardrobe and getting a bit more creative and conscious about what you want to wear and how you want to feel when you do. If today feels like a ball gown and glitter kinda day, why the hell not?

Travel is a huge mixer-upper and can allow us to gain new perspectives that we simply wouldn't get staying in the same place. I appreciate that jetting off across the world may not be a possibility depending on your current bank balance, but you could travel to the next town or even a different part of your own city or neighbourhood. We often forget to explore our local area and there's nothing more fabulous than discovering hidden gems just under your nose.

How about volunteering or starting a course? Following a passion can take you on all kinds of journeys and they don't even need to lead anywhere – the journey and the experience is all that is needed. When we begin to try new things it gives us new ideas and activities to talk and think about, and there's simply no space then for boredom or a colourless life.

Perhaps you *do* want bigger change, perhaps mixing it up for you is about quitting your job, starting your own business, moving to a new county or leaving your loveless relationship. There are times when we need to take our lives and shake them like a snow globe, turn them completely upside down and start from there. You're the only person who can decide what you need to feel alive and happy, but the ways to do so are limitless.

How to shake your life like Shakira shakes her hips!

1 **Shift your scenery** – go somewhere different, walk a new way to work, travel, eat somewhere new and take photos of the interesting things you see. If you're working from home, perhaps move to a new room or head to a coffee shop for a change of scenery.

2 **Boost your confidence** by trying something you've never done before (a class, a webinar, speed dating). It can be invigorating to push yourself away from the safety net of the ordinary. A quick internet search can reveal all kinds of wondrous events near where you live, and as our online life has exploded in the last few years the online options to try new things are plentiful.

3 **Write a bucket list** of brilliant things to do that would inspire, fulfil and energise you. Feel free to tag me on Instagram @iamhollymatthews or Twitter @hollymatthews as you tick things off your list so I can cheer you on and be inspired by your ideas.

‹**Don't underestimate the power of the tweak.** A little change can make all the difference.›

#5

Let's not be busy fools

Every time I see a post on social media with the slogan 'I'll sleep when I'm dead!' or I hear someone share how they 'hustled' on three hours' sleep to get to where they are, I don't feel inspired. I feel sick. What I see is the perfect guide to burnout and stress.

We live in a world where being busy is celebrated and seen as a mark of success, but I'm here to ruffle some feathers and stop the glorification of 'busy'. Being busy does not equal success. Having lots of fun and doing interesting things in your life is success, and mindless busyness should not be an ambition.

It's so easy to be busy in our daily lives without even trying. Work, meetings, social events, the endless housework, maybe you have a 'side hustle' or you're studying, or you're looking after a partner, kids or pets ... the list is endless. While we are trying to juggle the millions of life-balls we have flying in the air, we are missing what's actually going on around us and hurtling ourselves towards exhaustion.

Busy is not an achievement, it's the state of being preoccupied and scared. Scared you'll miss out, scared of failure, scared of facing emotions and, ultimately, scared you're not good enough.

Woah!

It's hard to hear 'busyness' described in this way, isn't it? We are all taught that being busy is a status symbol and a mark that we must be doing great. It's even become the thing we say as people ask how we are: 'Busy, busy!'

Let's see whether you fall into the category of 'busy, busy' by going through my little 'busy fools' checklist. You can nod along or grimace if you see yourself in each category. Let me note that I 100 per cent hit every category when I first realised the connection between busyness and fear, and it's something I am always fighting against. So you're not alone if you hit the 100 per cent club, too. Let's begin...

Do you feel guilty when you do nothing? Do you feel guilty for not being constantly 'on' or productive in some way? We have developed a horrible sense of shame around relaxing, as if taking our foot off the pedal to enjoy a moment somehow means we are worthless or lazy.

Are you a multitasking extremist who never does just one thing at a time? As a single mum of two, I constantly find myself doing 10 jobs at once and, even though this can sometimes feel like winning, studies have found that we are 40 per cent less effective at the tasks we are doing if we multitask, as our brains desperately switch from one job to the next.

Do you regularly get a bout of the FOMO (fear of missing out)? Then, rather than recognising and experiencing the feeling, you pack your days with things to do, busying your mind constantly to alleviate the worry that you might be missing something? This might also slip you into mindlessly scrolling through social media and checking out what everyone else is doing. I have definitely fallen into the hole of the zoned-out, glassy-eyed hour of scrolling through Instagram, suddenly finding myself looking at my friend's/sister's/cousin's holiday in Lanzarote in 2016, when I could be relaxing. I'm not judging you for doing this, but let's acknowledge our busy vices so we can keep them in check.

Do you find that rather than dealing with painful emotions you fill your life with 'busy' in order to avoid sitting with the darker moments? There can be a benefit in this, up to a point. I'm a big believer that we don't have to walk through our sadness or trauma in one fell swoop. That we can take bite-sized chunks out of our grief or loss and deal with things slowly. However, if you're not working through things in the background and *only* using busyness as your go-to way of coping then eventually this will cease to be helpful.

Do you wear 'busy' like a badge of honour? Do you almost look down on those that won't partake in the hustle and bustle of striving towards the next milestone? This was me (right before burnout), feeling all chuffed with myself that I was able to wake up early, miss lunch and stay up until midnight to build my 'best life'. Only I wasn't building my 'best life' – instead I was overloaded, unavailable and slaving away towards an unending and unquenchable thirst for the next 'thing'.

So how do you fare? Are you an emotion-avoiding, plate-spinning, never-switching-off busy fool or are you patting yourself on the back for being a chilled-out, breezy legend? Look, I fit firmly in the middle of these two camps and I'd imagine many of you do too. We are doing our best to slow down in a busy world that wants us to speed up and so, like everything in our quest for a happy life, we have to put some steps in place to help ourselves balance our worlds.

How to stop going faster and be more zen master

1 **Prioritise**. Work out what the most important values are in your life and prioritise doing more things that take you closer towards them, and lessen your time doing unnecessary tasks. At the start of each day, write down the *one* job that is your top priority that day and do that, well!

2 **Schedule in downtime**. For the person who is very goal orientated and is constantly striving to be their best self, I know that asking you to slow down will feel alien at first and so putting 'downtime' in your diary will help you to know this was a conscious decision, and not just a mindless moment of nothingness.

3 **Stop saying it!** Stop telling everyone you're busy as it reinforces the feeling of being busy. Instead, be intentional in your answer. When someone asks how you are, respond with something specific: 'I feel really good today, I have a meeting this morning and a lunch date with my friend this afternoon, so I've got lots to look forward to.' This feels a lot nicer than 'Crazy busy!'

4 **Pass it on**. Can you delegate some work to someone else? Can you teach your kids to do some chores? Can a friend run that errand? You don't have to be the doer of everything and even though we might get a kick out of the feeling of being everything to everyone, this will eventually lead to you being no help to anyone because you're too damn exhausted.

5 **Remind yourself you are amazing** regardless of how packed your day is, and focus on having more time to do nothing, guilt-free.

'Busy is not an achievement, it's the state of being preoccupied and scared.'

#6

No one is coming to save you

It would be truly lovely if every time we did something wrong, or something didn't feel quite right, we had someone else on hand to swoop in and wave a magic wand to fix it all. We have all had those moments when we'd like nothing more than to be put to bed and have someone else deal with our problems (and possibly feed us chocolate, too!).

As children, our parents may have been able to do that for us for a short time and this may have lulled us into a false sense of security. Then suddenly – WHAM! – we get thrown into the realities of adult life and find ourselves wondering what on earth is going on.

Truth bomb: you're on your own.

You mess up, you deal with it. Things get tough, you work it out. You leave the dishes by the sink, they'll still be there when you get back (infuriating, I know).

Coming to terms with this might feel a bit brutal at first (and many people find it easier to live in denial), but the quicker you accept that no one is coming to save you then the sooner you can begin to save yourself.

It's no one else's responsibility to make you happy. It's not your partner's job, or your children's, your parents' or your friends'. The more you look to outside intervention on your path to feeling great then the further away you will find yourself from your end goal.

I mean, of course, our friends and loved ones will hopefully be there to offer support where they can, but there's a huge difference between wanting to be around people and needing to be around them – needing people close to be your emotional pick-me-up every time there's a bump in the road is not the answer to long-term happiness.

Personal responsibility is a wonderful thing and the only way to feel truly fulfilled. Other people aren't here to fill a void in us; they're not tools to make us happy. If we start to expect this of others then, as soon as they drop the ball (which they will as they're human, remember?), you'll feel lingering dissatisfaction, and possibly find yourself beginning to resent them for not stepping up to the plate. No one can live up to these high expectations you have of them, and nor should you expect them to: it's selfish.

The sooner you can get to grips with the idea that if you do nothing, nothing happens, and if you wait around for others to change your life for you, STILL nothing happens, the quicker you can start to change your life for the better.

Fulfilment always begins with us being accountable for our own happiness, our own self-worth, our own self-validation. If we're not mindful of this then we might find ourselves waiting and waiting until it's game over and we realise we've allowed life to happen to us. We've been dragged from pillar to post without ever really making decisions ourselves or having taken control.

I don't want that for you, so it's time to stop waiting for the white knight and to be your own hero.

How do you escape the 'waiting for a fairy godmother' state of mind?

1 Check yourself (before you wreck yourself – you know you did it too!). Are you emotionally needy? Do you expect others to be there to champion you and lift you up? Are you waiting for the day when someone fixes things? Making time to reflect on these questions is an important starting point.

2 Get comfortable with being alone. Get to know yourself, learn to enjoy your own company, take yourself on a date. This could be a candle-lit dinner for one or perhaps it's trying a new class or learning a new skill. I love going to a coffee shop alone with a book or for a spot of people watching. Perhaps it's even grabbing the popcorn and going to watch a movie.

3 No blaming, no complaining. Rather than wasting your energy moaning about something that you would like to change, take action. Write a to-do list of the steps you need to take to create the change and get to work.

4 Remind yourself you don't have to ask permission to live a life you love. Don't waste time waiting for someone else to give you the go-ahead to create change.

5 Commit to owning your decisions, both your wins and your failures. The highs and lows of life are what shape us all, and by consciously deciding to own all our decisions – regardless of their outcomes – you will find a new sense of empowerment as you begin to steer your own ship.

'It's no one else's job to make you happy and you don't need them to.'

#7

Set big fat goals

In 2012, I was heavily pregnant with my daughter, Texas, and decided to set up an adult acting class. This largely came about because I wasn't able to go to auditions (while sporting a rather large baby bump) and so I had begun considering what else I could do to bring in some money. I had no business plan, no experience as a teacher, no venue and no idea if it would actually work.

After a conversation with a local actor, who informed me he was thinking about setting up a similar venture, I panicked that my idea would be taken. Within the hour, I had therefore rashly emailed a journalist from my local paper and told them they could run a story about my brand-new acting class. Less than a week later, I had everything I needed to start the class: a name, a venue, social media sorted, 15 students and a full-page article in a newspaper.

This was never in my 'big plan'. I didn't write it down in a bullet journal at the beginning of the year and create a step-by-step goal-setting strategy for how to achieve it. It just happened in the moment and on a whim.

So, when it comes to 'goal setting' I'm always torn. SMART goal setting (which we will discuss shortly) is undoubtedly beneficial, but some of what we get taught is a bit starry-eyed and sometimes might set us up to feel like total failures. I don't want you to feel like a failure. I *do* want you to achieve the things you'd like to achieve, so let's explore how we do that.

If you read books or articles by any of the big success coaches and business moguls you will notice that they mention SMART goals. This stands for:

- specific
- measurable
- achievable
- relevant
- time bound

But what do these actually mean? Let's break them down.

Specific is the difference between 'I want to earn more money' and 'I want to earn more money by gaining 10 new clients, who will work with me in a 1:1 capacity, within the next year.'

Measurable is the means by which you will know you have achieved your goal. The above example is very clear: 'I'll know because I'll have 10 new clients.'

Achievable is always a tricky one to define because sometimes when we aren't feeling very confident we set really tiny 'achievable' goals because they're low-hanging fruit and we know we can't fail. We do this because sometimes the big stuff we really want might feel beyond our grasp and daunting. Personally, when it comes to achievable, I try to think about it as a little check-in that we haven't gone wild and set a totally unrealistic goal, such as to make a million pounds within one month by working for 10 minutes a day.

Relevant is an interesting one and concerns how this goal is related to other goals or your 'bigger-picture goal'. If your bigger picture is to have a thriving coaching business with regular clients but you've started selling novelty mugs as well, I would argue that the novelty mugs (however fun they are) aren't relevant to the bigger plan.

Time bound is important since unless we put a time limit on things, we often just wait and don't do anything we have set out to do.

Now that I have explained the established thinking on goal setting, let me be real with you. SMART goals are boring. There you go, I've said it. They feel stale, corporate and cold. I get it, they make perfect sense when they're written down or explained in a presentation on a flip chart, but life just isn't really that straightforward. Life also includes changes of circumstances, impulsivity and heart.

Setting wildly 'unrealistic' goals can be exciting and brave, and some of my best ideas have been birthed from late-night musings and just getting stuff done. Don't confuse this with me not having a plan. There is a plan, but the plan is flexible and I know it might change at points.

> **'Setting wildly "unrealistic" goals can be exciting and brave.'**

My own bigger-picture life plan revolves around the freedom to do whatever I want, to be creative, to work around my children and to help others to live their version of that. Bearing this in mind, what does 'real goal setting' look like to me?

Each year and every month I chunk down my bigger-picture plan into SMART goals that will help make sure I stay on track and heading in the direction of the things I want. I then make room for 'hustle and heart'. Heart allows space for me to change course sometimes, based on my gut feelings, and hustle enables me to get things done when perhaps I don't feel like it that day.

This combination works for me, and could for you too. SMART goals will give you the on-paper 'ideal' road map, and 'hustle and heart' will allow you to trust the process, not obsess and keep taking action when you don't feel like it.

SMART goals will make you feel safe and organised, 'hustle and heart' will mean you jump in, you get brave and sometimes you start an acting class on a whim but still know it's part of the wider plan, even if it was a little unexpected detour.

To really have the life you want, I believe you have to give yourself the freedom to be flexible with the route towards that. You must also support that by creating great daily habits, working on all the limiting beliefs and self-sabotage behaviours that stopped you achieving this stuff before, and not being hard on yourself when life chucks a few roadblocks in your way, meaning you go a little off course. If you don't work on the mindset stuff along with the practicalities of achieving your goals then we will be back here on New Year's Day next year, opening up another journal and soullessly churning out yearly goals.

Working out who you need to become in order to achieve all of those sexy goals you wrote down is what's truly going to help you achieve them. Writing down 'how you do' stuff is easy; actually sticking to what needs to be done is what involves the internal mindset work.

How can I be SMART and have 'hustle and heart'?

1 **Create a list of all the things you'd like to achieve**. Big, small, scary and fun. Don't overthink this, just dump them all out and make sure you're thinking about what that 'ideal' life would look and, most importantly, feel like.

2 **Sort 'em out**. Look at the brain dump and write out more specific goals, such as 'I want to climb Mount Everest by the time I'm 40.' Next to each, write why you'd like to do this: 'Because climbing a mountain would be cool and I'll have to get fit to do that, so health wise it'll be nice too.'

3 **Date 'em**. Work out which goals are doable in the next few weeks and months, which ones are yearly, and which will require a few stages and may take five or even 10 years to achieve.

4 **Talk about 'em**. Tell other people about these goals. This will hold you accountable and make it much more attainable. There's nothing like a little peer pressure to motivate us.

5 **Think about 'em (but not too much)**. Think about and visualise how you will feel as you tick off these goals, but don't obsess about them. Obsessing and fussing tells your subconscious that you don't really believe you can achieve them.

#8

You're being a bully to yourself

Let's imagine you have a friend who is extremely critical. She's the friend who points out your flaws, judges your house decor, mentions the weight you've gained and knocks your confidence at every turn. I'm sure you've experienced one of these people in your lifetime (you've got someone in your head right now, haven't you?), so you know that being on the receiving end of this kind of daily jabbing is horrible.

I'm pretty confident, though, that after a few of their carefully dropped nasty comments, and generally not feeling too amazing around them, you've removed this person from your life or at the very least had less to do with them. Now here's the point: if we won't accept this kind of behaviour from someone else, why on earth do we accept it from our own brains?

We have a constant stream of thoughts in our mind and these are both positive and negative. At certain times in our lives, though, the voice of negativity and sneering judgement can be pretty damn loud. This voice is often referred to as the 'inner critic', but you are more than welcome to give it your own name (Negative Norman, Sneaky Suzy or Crappy Colin have come up as suggestions from clients in my workshops).

Now people could very easily confuse their inner critic with the truth or their conscience, but this is not the case. The inner critic is not about you being self-aware or self-reflective. Instead, the inner critic is unnecessary, demeaning and overly harsh. It is not based on truth. It is the voice that tells you 'you're ugly', 'no one likes you', 'you'll never get the job' and other such unfounded statements.

The problem is that we can become so used to this stream of demotivating chatter that we forget it's there; it becomes a programme that is secretly running underneath the surface and affecting what we do in our daily lives. If, every time we try to make a positive decision, we hear the inner voice of doom telling us 'You'll do a rubbish job, you always do', then feeling brave enough or good enough to do anything at all begins to feel like climbing a mountain.

Having encountered many a bully in my time, I have learned that the only way to stop them is to confront and deal with them. This doesn't always mean going head to head – sometimes it requires pacifying or reasoning. Either way, it is essential that we face up to and handle the situation. Things are no different when it comes to our own venomous inner critic: we have to call it out and hear it out.

The words that our 'inner fault finder' uses are potentially something we decided about ourselves a long time ago, often as far back as childhood. Maybe the words that we now repeat on loop inside our heads are words that were spoken to us by someone else, which we took on as truth. As these beliefs about ourselves have often been around for some time, it does take a little work to shut them up and change them into something kinder and more productive. So how do we do this?

In reality, our inner critic *is* us and it's behaving in the way it is because it's trying to protect us from potential failure or rejection. It's perhaps encountered the feeling of loss or embarrassment and doesn't fancy going through that again. So how about before we vilify and shout down this inner voice, we befriend and understand its point of view. Start here: really listen to the inner critic, hear the words that are on loop, begin noticing how brutal these words can be and give them some air time. This might all sound a bit contradictory when our goal here is to get you to stop picking on yourself, but first you need to know what you're dealing with.

Next up, explore where you might have heard this voice before. The school teacher who said you were useless because you happened to find maths challenging (and it was their area of expertise); the boy who laughed at your acne-prone skin with his friends and made you want to hide under your quilt for a week (this is a personal one of mine and it took me years to begin liking my face, thanks a bunch Josh!). Whoever or wherever the voice in your head took its inspiration from, start understanding its origin and be kind enough to yourself to recognise that you don't have to repeat the words any more.

Now we've got to know the backstory and heard a bit about why these words have ended up in our heads, it's time for you to put on the gloves and fight back. For every mean sentence you heard 'Negative Norman' utter, find a counterargument or proof that the opposite is true. When Norman says, 'You're useless at everything!' I want you to counter this with a list of things you have at some point done well, or at least times when you've certainly not done a *useless* job.

What about the amazing meal you cooked last year that everyone raved about? The kids' Halloween costumes you knocked up out of toilet rolls and a black bin bag? How about the fact you're an adult human being who runs a household, puts petrol in the car and functions day to day? This is not light work and goes in the pile of proof that you are far from useless.

The greatest way to challenge the bully that is your inner critic is to take action. Keep showing up for yourself until you realise that your inner critic just hasn't been all that loud lately. We need to teach our brains to believe in us again and that comes from doing something to prove our negative voice wrong. We have to fight for ourselves and we have to stop allowing this voice to run amok any time it wants.

How to shut up the negative voice

1 **Notice the voice**. What are the words and daily put-downs used? Explore where they came from. Pinpoint the source.

2 **Challenge the voice**. Every time the negative thoughts pop up, ask yourself the following: Is this a true statement? Is this my own thought or did I get this from someone else? Is this thought helping me and serving me well?

3 **Fight back**. Get out a pen and paper and write down 20 counterarguments to the negative voice. Keep this list with you and whip it out when you need that daily reminder that you are awesome (perhaps even ask friends and loved ones to contribute to the list).

4 **Take action**. What can you do today that is *you* showing up for *you*? Take one step closer to a goal you have or make one kind gesture to yourself. Don't overcomplicate this as the inner critic loves to turn things into a big deal. You know better than the voice. Just take a step.

'Your inner critic is not your conscience. Take action and prove this negative voice wrong.**'**

#9

You're amazing (a pep talk)

Do you know what? Life is really flipping hard sometimes and feeling good about it can feel like wading through treacle. We live in a world where the media fills us with fear, we have to pay bills, be a good friend, go to work, maybe look after others, and also try to look presentable. With all of these expectations we can spend our days feeling 'less than' and not good enough.

How miserable is that?

So, this is me reminding you (and myself) that we are enough. In fact, we are more than enough, we are downright excellent and I am sick of the feelings that contradict these statements. Let's look at the science behind this to back up what I'm saying...

Put it this way, just being alive is pretty astounding. Do you have any idea of the complexities of human biology that have to come together in order for you to be in this world? I mean I'm fairly confident you know about the birds and the bees and the functional way you were 'made', but have you actually thought about what has to happen so that every component aligns to create a human being. It's a lot! You've beaten all sorts of odds to get here.

For instance, in order to make a baby, a man has to produce sperm, of which just one in a million reaches and fertilises an egg and develops into an embryo. You are literally one in a million. When you think about it like that, don't you feel like you deserve a prize? I think you do. I feel like coming to your home, shaking your hand and saying, 'Well done you, you're here, you did great!'

Now I am aware that the current perception of modern living is that 'everyone thinks they deserve a prize for being alive' and I have just played directly into that stereotype, but I'm not saying you should stop there and continue to congratulate yourself for being alive while contributing nothing else to society.

This moment of making your entrance into the world was just the beginning and I have no doubt that since this time you have added value to the world, and also dealt with many challenges. What's more, contrary to the above accusation that some modern humans expect a prize just for breathing, I actually think that most of us hear and internalise negative things about ourselves more often than we get a pat on the back.

So beyond the science, let's think more about why you're simply brilliant. How about the fact that I know you have been through some difficult times. I don't know what your particular brand of difficulty is, but I guarantee you didn't pick this book up because everything has gone exactly as planned. You've likely experienced losses and pain and sadness, possibly break-ups and health issues, people may have been really mean to you and you might have failed over and over again.

You have gone through a ton of stuff that has been challenging and hard and yet here you are. You're amazing and I really am going to unashamedly gush about you because I also know that the likelihood is that you're often far from kind to yourself in your own head.

If you find yourself doubting yourself today, remind yourself of this: the world needs you. In your own personal part of this planet, you add value and make the world a better place, every single day. You help out other people, you might be a valued colleague, perhaps you bring humour or honesty to your circle of friends and family. Those around you rate your energy highly and you bring a little something into this world in a way that only you can.

No more hiding your light, keeping ideas to yourself or talking about yourself in any way other than positive. Quite frankly it's boring and we aren't here long enough to spend our days hating ourselves. I know you did all that stuff that you regret and wish you could change.

I know that while I call you 'amazing' you're meticulously trawling through thoughts of the time when you messed something up and didn't achieve some accolade or milestone you think you should have. I know you're getting ready to contradict my explicit praise, but I know all of this and yet it makes no difference. Say it again: you are amazing.

I may need a little work on feeling amazing, how can I do this?

1 **Ask others what your best qualities are**. You can even use this book as a lead-in if you feel uncomfortable doing this: 'I'm reading this book right now and the author has set me a challenge to ask people I know about my best qualities.' You can cringe all you want as you ask and even call me names for challenging you (I'll take this hit, it's worth it). Once you get a lovely long list, save it somewhere. Refer to it when you're feeling less than amazing and your brain is tricking you into doubting yourself. We can call this your 'I am awesome folder'. I'd love you to share with me what kind words you hear.

2 **Create a list of your people**. These are the energisers, not the drains, and the ones you need for different reasons. Your 'my people' list should consist of 'the person who makes you laugh', 'the logical friend', 'the person you go to when you're sad', 'the person you can rely on when you need a favour', 'the friend who really believes in you and somehow makes you believe in yourself'. If your

current team needs a little work, you now know what you want and can start building that support network for when you need reminding of your fabulousness.

3 **Remind yourself of the times you had a setback but then worked it out**. Grab a pen and paper and create three columns. In the left-hand column write 'The thing that happened', in the middle one write 'How I dealt with it' and finally in the right-hand column 'The lessons'. Doing this for a few of your mishaps or difficult times will allow you to see what a great human you are and how clever you were to work through all those things.

'The world needs you. In your own personal part of the planet, you add value and make the world a better place.'

#10

Don't give up

On more than one occasion in my life I have been described as 'relentless'. Now, of course, I am very sure that on the occasions when this tag has been pinned to me it has not always been meant in a positive way, but I personally choose to take it as a positive.

I am relentless.

When I want something I will try, fall down, get up, try again, be a bit bruised from the first fall and keep going. More often than not, this relentless approach serves me extremely well. Certainly in the acting world, you have to have that 'never give up' kind of nature, because the chances of you getting the very few parts on offer are slim and you will hear 'no' more than I care to think about (even when you're succeeding). The unfortunate truth is that many people will give up just before their 'luck' is about to change – they will get so close and then for one reason or another they will decide to stop.

Don't misunderstand my dogged approach, however, and take it to mean 'keep doing the same thing over and over again'; evolving and adapting is an important ingredient when it comes to 'never giving up'. The lessons and the journey are all part of you getting to the dizzy heights that most won't achieve.

I love gritty people (see 'How to have unshakable grit' on p. 226 to find out more). I love to hear stories of people who have challenged convention and pushed themselves beyond what they initially thought was possible. They excite me and inspire me and what I love most is that these people are rarely extraordinary; they are just people who wouldn't give up and were willing to go the extra mile.

There will be times in your life, though, when the chips are down, when events around you cause you to slip into a space where you want to give up. Those moments when you've had enough and you don't think you can give any more are tough (I'm with you, my friend, I've been there, too, and it's no fun).

I remember one particular night about eight months after the death of my husband and having not long been in my new home. My daughters, who were aged around five and seven, were both screaming and crying in my bed. One was angry, one was desperately sad and I was in the middle trying to calm both. I myself had had a rough and emotional day and felt like I had no energy to give, as hour after hour this chaos continued around me.

There was a moment in that when I thought 'I can't do this on my own.' I was scared, frustrated and felt suffocated. However, after a while, both girls' emotions calmed and as the tears still leaked down my face, they cuddled into me tightly. Even though I was drained and sad I tapped into our innate human strength and allowed this moment to pass.

So, even though our circumstances are inevitably different, you and I have this in common: the core of the human body and mind wants to survive and wants to thrive, so even when we hit our most desperate moments we can tap into a deeper level of ourselves and cling on.

I was trying to think about how we do this and what it is that keeps us going and it suddenly hit me in its simplicity – it's hope. It's the hope of a better day and a brighter future. We hope that one day we will find love, the right job, the perfect home, a happier moment.

Even in your darkest times, you might find that the 'hope' that has been lying dormant in the pit of your stomach surfaces and drags you along, keeps you going. Hope is tenacious and fierce, it's the survivor in you that gets people through cancer diagnoses, grief, relationship break-ups and every moment of despair. I talk about it more in 'Some days are crap' on p. 166.

Sadly, some of you feel ready to give up right now. Frankly, this makes me very glad that you're reading this because it means that perhaps I can give you some food for thought and you might tap into your inner powerhouse and keep going.

I'd like that. You're important and we need you. You might be one step away from victory and you will never know that unless you keep walking.

How to keep going when you want to give up

1 **Find a supportive tribe**. When people go through alcoholism and drug recovery, one of the main healing tools is having support and a community. I think we all need this. I know from my own experience of building an online community that when people feel like giving up, the group will rise to the occasion and hoist that person in the air. Your support network will have your back when you forget to. Your group or your tribe might not be the people you're surrounded by right now, and you may have to go and find those who are on the same path. We're mega lucky though because we live in the age of the internet where it is easier than ever to find a loving space to bed down. You're already part of my gang and I have the best network of caring souls in my Facebook group (www.facebook.com/groups/thehappymeproject) that will scoop you up and give you a safe place to land.

2 **Find a different how**. You have to become a little more loosey-goosey about how you get to the things you want. You set a goal, then if you go at it one way and it doesn't work out, perhaps there's another route to the same outcome. Understand that the discoveries you'll have along the journey are part of the magic of life and if we got everything we wanted, the moment we wanted it, I'm not sure

we would fully appreciate what we had. Stay open to change and evolution. Adaptability is key.

3 **Watch someone else do something 'impossible'**. For every time we feed ourselves the stories of this being 'the end' for us or that we will never have something, there is someone else out there smashing down walls to success. Go on YouTube, grab a book and look for 'famous failures' or people who have survived when the odds were stacked against them. Knowing that it can be done is sometimes half the battle. Your inspiration doesn't have to come from people you know: the world is large and full of people who keep going even when that seems impossible.

4 **Change your space**. Change your location, mix things up and even change your posture. We can get stuck in one mindset and only see things from one perspective. By literally changing the things you see, you can open up the imagination and the solution-finding parts of your brain. If you can, do a headstand or handstand (I appreciate this is slightly niche), as there is a definite benefit in seeing the world upside down for a moment, plus it sends a rush of blood to the head and fires up your muscles, which releases feel-good chemicals.

'Even in your darkest moments you might find that the "hope" that has been lying dormant in the pit of your stomach surfaces and forces you to keep going.'

#11

Be weird

In a world in which we are more aware of other people's lives than ever before, and a young girl in Coventry can tell you the latest fashion fads in Milan, it's easy for us to start becoming a collective, all following and doing the same stuff. This is often because very early on in our lives we learn that being different equals being weird, and being weird means being left out.

As a young child, I was weird. I loved to perform and was always very creative. I went through a phase of wearing tights on my head as I thought it looked like long hair and I had no issues with standing out from the crowd. Fast-forward to high school and I realised that all the quirks that had been celebrated and applauded in primary school would now make me a social outcast. Overnight, I began to try to fit in.

I quit playing the guitar because I was too embarrassed to carry it to school. I so desperately wanted to be like my friends, but on the inside I knew that a lot of my ambitions and dreams were very different to those of the people around me. Getting my first TV acting job at 11 meant I was instantly pegged as different, and even as I clawed my way towards blending into the crowd (because of our crippling need for societal approval), I didn't quite succeed and this often left me feeling like an inadequate alien playing by rules I didn't or couldn't understand.

These days, by contrast, I embrace and love all my weirdness. I also teach my daughters to stand out from the crowd, to be 'a flamingo in a flock of pigeons' because being your truest, realest self is the most liberating thing you can do. When you step into your weird and set it free into the world, you begin to attract your very own band of weirdos to hang out with.

The wonderful thing about the internet and social media is that there truly is nothing so weird that someone else isn't already doing or enjoying it, and with a little research suddenly you can connect with another person or even a whole community who understands your 'weird'. Maybe that will become a wonderful friendship or perhaps even a deep love affair, but either way, you certainly won't feel alone.

Truly, though, what is normal anyway? It's a very subjective topic and finding your weird means owning all of who you are and being authentic to who that is. Copycat behaviour only ever leaves you being a poor version of someone else, when you can be the best version of yourself.

Many of us are inspired by people all the time – for example, we might follow our favourite celebrities and imitate aspects of who they are. This is perfectly fine, normal and a great way to learn. If, however, we begin to slip into the realm of thinking we have to be exactly like [insert the name of the person you most like to stalk online], we end up feeling a bit deflated and miss the glaringly obvious fact that no one can compete with us when we are ourselves, because that is completely unique to us.

So, let's talk about you for a second... How are you odd, weird or different? What are the things that make you stand out and that you have perhaps even been made fun of for in the past? Whatever they are, these traits (if you allow them) can become your superpower, the things that make you exceptional and the things that, through embracing them, help you to feel connected to others and to who you really are.

You're not a mediocre person, even on the days when you feel like you might be, and I know that once you start on this journey of self-discovery you're going to say, 'Damn, I am a peculiar, interesting, lovely, weirdo. And all of that is OK with me.' And that's what I want.

Conformity will keep you in a box and it will stop you growing. The greatest minds in the world were often first laughed at for being kooky or off the wall. The greatest art, inventions and change happens when people go against the grain, when they step out of the line and do something renegade.

How to own your weird

1 **Identify what sets you apart**, or the true fundamentals of who you are. Are you someone who just loves to collect trainers, or who spends hours and hours drawing, painting or writing poetry? Are you someone who enjoys nothing more than pickles on toast or who relaxes by listening to ASMR (the whispery voice stuff you find on YouTube and Spotify that some people really, really love)? Whoever you are and whatever you like is valid and makes you, you. Grab a pen and write a list, make a poster or just reflect for a moment on the offbeat little things that shape your uniqueness.

2 **Embrace your weird**. Now you know what your unique qualities are, it's time to open your arms and embrace your eccentricities (even the ones you've been hiding away all these years). The fact is, you are a bloody miracle, all humans are. How we came to be here, walking around and living our lives is simply incredible. By shying away from what makes you stand out, you are limiting your wonderful potential.

3 **Connect with people who have similar interests**. I meet lots of people who tell me they are doing something they love, but no one around them 'gets it'. I tell them it's perfectly fine that their friends or family don't get it but that they need to find people to express that side of themselves to: their gang. Your challenge is to join a group, class or forum and seek out those whom you can jam with. There's nothing wrong with being a lone wolf but it's certainly nice to feel connection.

4 **STOP telling yourself you're not good enough** (we might say this a lot in this book!). You are good enough, you're perfectly imperfect and that includes all your 'quirks' – such as the fact that you are obsessed with Gary Barlow, you don't wear shoes, you choose to dye your hair a different colour every month, or perhaps a combination of all of these! Everything is acceptable, it's *your* life.

"Being your truest and realest self is the most liberating thing you can do."

#12

Don't take yourself so seriously

Lying on the ground in Epping Forest, Essex, and acting like an otter is up there as one of the strangest things I have ever done (although if I'm honest, it still doesn't hit the top spot).

This moment in my life occurred while I was attending East 15 Acting School – one of the most prestigious drama schools in the UK. During this particular lesson I was getting in touch with the animal in order to then use its movement and vibe to develop a human character.

I know, I know. You're reading this thinking, 'Holly, you were rolling around in the mud in a forest, acting like an otter with friends. It's weird.' I hear you and, as I lay there, there was a moment when I took myself out of the 'actor' in me and thought about how this would look to anyone with a 'proper job'. I knew it would appear odd, but I also knew that in that moment my biggest concern was that we were doing this exercise in a location that really wasn't proper otter terrain. I mean, where was the water?

Being an actor forces you to not take yourself seriously. I should clarify: actors tend to take the work itself very seriously, but if you are going to be prancing around in a costume pretending for a living, you have to see the absurdity of that too.

As little kids, we love to play and pretending comes easily to most. Children commonly act out being fairies and wizards and will decide at any given moment that they want a new name and possibly even a cape and a sword. They don't attach any social stigma to that and they live with a freedom that we spend our adulthood chasing.

As grown-ups, we stop playing. We become rigid and inflexible in our thinking. We fear judgement and we step into control mode. But when we let go and laugh at our mistakes and quirks, and even lean into them, we feel our shoulders drop and sigh with a sense of relief. It's so much easier to laugh through life than to think we have to have it all figured out.

My friend Emma Stroud is a clown. This isn't a judgement of her as a person, she is an actual real-life, professional clown. She is also an MC, speaker and founder of Laugh. Think. Play. She said to me:

> 'Humour and laughter are the biggest expressions of humanity we have. When we allow ourselves to truly laugh and connect to our joy, we know how good it feels. Yet there is a fear, a resistance as adults that laughter, joy, play and silliness is just not "adult enough". That to be an adult we must be serious. When and how did this become a rule? Allow yourself to play more, be curious and notice how much lighter you feel. It is the light that we all have access to, all of the time. Allow it.'

How could we not agree? However, actually giving yourself permission to step into your 'silly' is harder than in looks. Although I wholeheartedly believe in jumping into the farcical side of life, this doesn't mean I haven't been caught out by the need to please and felt pressured to show up in a way I felt I was 'supposed to' on occasion.

For instance, when I first started out as a 'businesswoman' I thought that meant I had to leave behind the ludicrous things I had done in the past. There was a moment, and I have to say it was just a moment, when I was looking at the clichéd example of a serious adult 'businesswoman' and thinking this is what I had to become to succeed. The actor in me had tapped into what the role of a 'businesswoman' needed to look like: it resembled a lawyer in the TV show Suits, and she most definitely had some sort of folder that she must use to carry around 'very important stuff'. Thankfully, a few good mentors and friends had a few strong words to say to me about this, and reminded me that I can be a 'businesswoman' and still be playful and goofy.

Letting down your guard, being vulnerable and childlike has some proven health benefits too. It lowers stress and helps us cope with the tough moments in life better, and you'll build better relationships with those around you. My husband Ross would regularly say, 'Those who play together, stay together' and I believe this completely. In fact, when we talk about the 'spark' going out in a relationship it's often because we have forgotten how to laugh with each other and our focus has become fixated on the negative and the mundane.

Being in a play mindset can help you be more creative and less rigid in your thinking. It can nudge you out of your comfort zone and tumble you into new spaces. Who knows, with a play mindset, we could see you starting your own gospel choir, trying out burlesque or at the very least learning to laugh and smile once more.

Clowning around doesn't mean you're an inferior adult. It means you are an adult who respects themself enough to allow themself to enjoy life, and who recognises that even if you do everything you are 'supposed' to do, there are still going to be things that happen that are utterly ridiculous and there is nothing you can do about that, apart from laugh.

Hit me up with some playtime ideas, I'm ready to clown

1 **Get messy**. Recently, my children were bored and irritating each other and although there was torrential rain outside, I needed to get them out in the fresh air to let off some steam. I knew it was going to be a mudfest, so we put on our scruffy clothes and wellies, tied up our hair and went to the park. I had factored in us all being a mess and

so at the park I rolled down a hill. The kids howled with laughter, I felt a release of tension (although I'm in my late 30s, so I felt nauseous for about 20 minutes afterwards too), and we had a wonderful time. Find ways to allow the mess – to make slime, salt dough, a mud kitchen – and to let go.

2 **Get creative**. It doesn't matter if you're any good, get out the paintbrushes and give it a go. Sketch, knit, cut and stick, and if you're feeling very 'out there', slap on the eco-friendly glitter (I mean, you'll regret the glitter almost instantly because it will live in your house forever, but hey, at least every guest who comes to your home will remember you, right?).

3 **Dance**. Wriggle, move, stretch, twerk, shake those hips and throw those shapes. Who cares if you're actually any good? I'm not asking you to take it up as a profession, I'm asking you to lighten up and loosen up. Start your morning by blasting your favourite tunes and dancing boldly around your house.

4 **Stop worrying about what others think of you**. As I write this I'm sitting in my car (waiting for my kids to finish their gymnastics lesson) and there are two 10-years-olds perched on a wall to the right of my window. They're laughing loudly, playing the fool, have taken off their shoes and couldn't care less about my opinion of what they're doing. I love it! Be more like these girls and stop assuming everyone is watching or cares what you're doing.

'It's so much easier to laugh through life than to think you have it all figured out.'

#13

Gratitude is a game changer

Every single mindset coach, psychologist, therapist and religious leader is going to at some point talk about gratitude. We aren't clones, there are just some things that are universal truths and you cannot skip them on your journey into happiness.

Now I understand that the pessimistic among you may have read the word 'gratitude' and internally (or externally!) rolled your eyes, but give me this chapter to win you round and show you how the big G will make your life better.

Let me be bold for a minute here and say that gratitude changed my life, and possibly even saved it. Some really awful things have happened to me over the last 10 years – life-changing, tragic, painful moments that I would have done anything to stop from happening. What allowed me to move through these times and give myself respite was noticing the moments of good around the bad.

When I am working with clients and gratitude comes up, I have found that they can be very resistant to the idea of practising feeling grateful when they're in their darkest moments. I get it, of course, because feeling grateful as you lose your job or when you've just found out your husband is cheating on you is a hard thing to do, and I do not suggest that you offer the idea of gratitude up to someone as advice when they are wading through the peak of their hardship.

However, there simply *is* always something to feel grateful for. You don't have to feel grateful for the thing you don't want to be happening, but sitting right next to the painful things are moments, people and pockets of time to feel grateful for. Cling on to these to aid your healing. And check out 'What if it were all taken?' on p. 260 for more ideas.

When my husband and I found out he had brain cancer we felt grateful for many things. Not brain cancer, of course, brain cancer is crap, but we felt grateful that we live in a country where he could get free healthcare, support and access to amazing doctors. We felt grateful that we had children, that we had a home, for the support of friends and family, that we had created flexible working lives that meant we could make things work around his treatment, and we felt extremely grateful for each other.

By grasping at the stuff surrounding our pain we were able to change our focus, meaning that even with cancer dictating a lot of our life at that time, it didn't have all of us.

That, of course, is my own personal experience and is purely anecdotal. But Professor Robert Emmons, an expert in gratitude, has studied its impact on our lives and believes it's fundamental to us getting through tough times and being happier more than we are sad. He believes gratitude is 'vital' in times of adversity, and I wholeheartedly agree.

Another argument that's commonly used against the practice of gratitude is that it can keep us stuck in some floaty, living-in-the-now, not-caring-about-the-future limbo, and can effectively make us lazy or complacent about life. Some believe that if they feel grateful for the right now (at least some of it), it will kill their motivation to want or be more.

I call BS on this. Thankfully, this is backed up by the results of studies conducted by Robert Emmons and his colleagues at the University of California (and it's always good to have the backing of science, right?).

They studied three groups for 10 weeks and told them to pick six goals across all aspects of their lives. They then instructed the first group to practise being grateful, the second to focus on daily annoyances and the third to note what affected them (without a focus on positive or negative) every day during the test period. When the results were in, they were able to discern a 20 per cent increase in the first group's progress towards their goals, and even saw that this first cohort made fewer trips to the doctor than the other two groups. So, it seems that being grateful can increase productivity and perhaps even benefit your health.

For me, though, the biggest factor in why it works is that we know that if you keep telling yourself the world is a terrible place and focus your attention on this at length, your brain is going to assume you want more evidence to back up these negative thoughts. By contrast, if you feed in grateful thoughts, your focus will be on those and your brain will bring to your attention more things to feel grateful about. (For more on this see 'How the brain works' on p. 16.)

Happy people talk about what they feel grateful for and what they love in specific detail. It's rarely a generic gratitude, it's 'I feel grateful to you for making me breakfast this morning, the egg was done to perfection and it was wonderful to be cooked for.' Or 'I feel so grateful to have a lie-in this morning, my bed is so comfy and warm.'

Kids are amazing at practising gratitude and if you have children (or can borrow a few – with permission, of course) then ask them what they feel grateful for or what they love about their lives and they will likely wow you with their gratitude skills. 'I feel grateful for my socks,' declared my youngest daughter on one of our Monday morning gratitude walks (a walk during which we simply take turns to state what we are feeling grateful for in that moment). 'I feel grateful for our neighbours,' said my oldest. You see, kids notice the finer details and the moments that us adults can take for granted. I think that we must begin to appreciate and notice in that same childlike manner, because gratitude truly is a game changer.

I'm ready to feel happy and grateful, where do I start?

1 **Set a reminder**. It's easy to feel very ungrateful about having to get out of your bed (especially if you have to get up early or are woken by your children asking things like 'Mum, you know *everything*, how does this work?'), so set a reminder on your phone and label it 'feel grateful'. It's a very simple tip but it works.

2 **Find your time**. Whether it's while you're brushing your teeth, during the car journey to work or putting on your make-up, pick a time to actively recite in your mind the things you feel grateful for.

3 **Use the magic reframe word: 'get'**. 'I get to do my dishes', 'I get to take out the bins'. By changing the word 'have' to 'get' you recognise how lucky you are. Taking the bins out is my least favourite job, but when I change 'have' to 'get' I am able to recognise that if I 'get' to take out the bins then this means I have a house, I have food and stuff to put in a bin, and I'm phsycially capable of performing the task. As I live in a house, I am warm and likely to have clothes on my back.

'Sitting right next to our painful moments is something to feel grateful for – cling to this to help change your focus.'

#14

Saying 'yes' when you mean 'hell no!'

Picture the scene. You're in the school playground dropping off your kids. Becky (with the good hair) sashays over and asks whether you could look after her son Zach for an hour after school. She's smiling, warm, practically begging, and you find yourself saying 'yeah, sure' and then checking if Zach is allergic to anything so you can make him a nutritious and wholesome dinner.

Now this situation may seem like a lovely exchange of kindness and support, one mum helping out another. But let's say this isn't the first time you've done this. Let's say Becky is often late and the hour drags on into the night, sometimes even with a little sleepover thrown into the mix. Let's say lovely Zachary isn't so lovely and having him at your home creates absolute carnage, leaving you picking crisps out of your rug for a week. So, when Becky initially asks, alarms go off in your head and you internally scream 'NO' as your mouth betrays you.

We say 'yes' many times in our lives when we really want to say 'no', but why?

I think it's that we generally want to be nice so that we're liked. Simple, right? We try to treat others as we would like to be treated. We think about how we would feel if we were asking someone for a favour and how grateful we'd be if they agreed.

We say 'yes' because we don't want the person to not like us, for us to be rejected in some way. We have an inbuilt fear of being pushed out of a group and so our subconscious is always on the lookout to protect us from that. We're scared that if we say 'no' then an argument will ensue and we'll have to leave the friendship circle, and be isolated and alone.

If we're of a particularly anxious mindset we may even escalate this further still, imagining that a 'no' will lead to a public brawl. When your brain is offering up these intrusive thoughts it seems a reasonable reason to just say 'yes', right?

But when we habitually say 'yes', like an annoying people-pleasing tic, we end up agreeing to so much that we can find ourselves running from place to place while not really doing anything to the best of our ability. We drop balls all over the place and eventually burn out while getting annoyed with the people to whom we said 'yes' in the first place. Poor Becky has no idea that the 'yes' you offered up came through gritted teeth and inadvertently made her public enemy number one in your eyes.

It is not other people's job to keep us in check. Everyone is just trying to get by. Some people are more confident in asserting what it is that they want, and some may even manipulate those around them who are less confident into doing things for them. Your internal anger will do nothing to stop you being taken advantage of. What will help you is boundaries.

Boundaries are key to a happy life. Training people around you to understand what your boundaries and 'rules' are is fundamental; we have to learn to speak up and be upfront about what we want and what we definitely do not want.

I'm aware that milder characters may feel nervous about this, and I get it because I was you once too. I said 'yes' to so much that didn't sit well with me and it wasn't good for me in the long run. I'm still working on this lesson but the more I say 'no' to the drinks I don't want to attend, the more space I create to say 'yes' to the things I do want.

Boundaries help in my professional life, too. I'm a helper by nature and what drives me to be a coach is the desire to help, but I cannot help others fully if I'm just doing things for them or swooping in to 'fix' their life. For this reason, I've created big fat boundaries when it comes to how I work, and the stronger my boundaries, the more headspace I have to create work that can help more people. If we spread ourselves too thinly, we end up helping no one and resenting the ones we do. You can be a compassionate and empathic human being while also not being a pushover.

How to say 'no' and feel OK about it

1 **Ask yourself honestly if this is something you want to do**. Then answer from a place of truth, not through a veil of being the 'good' person. Decide on your hard nos, the things you simply won't do. Create boundaries around these, making sure they're not blurry, and consider what you will do if and when someone crosses them.

2 **Say 'I am enough. I am valuable. My opinions matter.'** to yourself on loop. Stop putting yourself last. You can't pour from an empty cup and you need to train that brain of yours to believe that you must come first.

3 **Stand tall**. When you say 'no', stand tall and plant your feet or sit confidently in your chair. Maintain eye contact and focus on your breath if nerves are rearing their ugly head. Be clear, direct and honest with your words.

4 **Don't use qualifiers or apologetic talk**, such as 'I'm sorry but I'm not totally sure I'm comfortable with that, perhaps I don't

understand fully.' Instead, say, 'I'm not comfortable with that.' Feel the difference. Neither is rude, one is just far more direct and honest. Understand too that 'No.' is a full sentence and doesn't have to come with a stream of excuses after it. Just 'No.'

5 **Flex your 'no' muscle**. This is something you may need to practise – it's a skill to be learned, a craft even. My challenge to you is to say 'no' to one thing this week. Start small and work your way up. 'No I won't pay for lunch again, let's go halves,' for example, or 'No I won't stay an hour late at work for the third time this week to help you out.' Remember that saying 'no' now is better than being resentful later.

❝Say "no" to the things you don't want, so you can say "yes" to the things you do.❞

#15

What does your ideal life look like?

A few years ago, when my youngest daughter Texas was five, I asked her what she would like to be when she grew up. Her answer, without a blink, was 'the tooth fairy'. She could tell me what she'd look like, where she'd live and how she would feel. There was no doubt or fear, just a comfortable and very cute acceptance of what would be and what she wanted.

If I asked her the same question now she would say 'a gymnast' with the same lack of doubt and strength of vision, not worrying for a second whether I would judge her or if the change in direction implies something about her.

When was the last time you asked yourself what you wanted from life or considered who you are right now? When did you last acknowledge that your life could look exactly as you want it to and that once you have decided what a 'good life' is for you, you can begin creating it.

We have a choice. I know it doesn't always feel like it when we're right in the middle of a tough time or we've taken ourselves down a path (sometimes through no fault of our own) from which getting out seems impossible, but even in our darkest moments there are ways to wriggle through the mud and bloom in a way that suits you right now.

I want you to begin asking yourself questions that help you to explore who you are today and what you would like your life to look like in this moment. Don't focus on what you thought it was going to look like or the thing you think would be easiest or rock the boat the least. Think about the actual, real-life goals and wants you have *now*.

Where would you like to live? Who would you like to be around? What would you like to do as a job? How would you like to show up every day? Allow yourself a moment to start imagining and playing out scenarios in your mind (we call this 'visualisation') and just see what comes up for you.

You see, we don't have to be the same version of ourselves forever. In fact, if you remain the same throughout your life then I would argue you haven't lived at all.

After a particularly difficult time in my life, I began working with a business coach who asked me what days and times I would like to work on my business. Having always been a self-employed person I'd always considered myself someone who understood I had choice and could live my life in a way that worked for me, but I realised I had never considered this choice (if I'm honest, I just worked constantly). After that conversation I looked at when I was most productive and when I had space to work around my kids, and it really made me reassess things.

Unfortunately, people in the past may well have dismissed your ideas about what your life could look like, telling you to be more 'realistic' and to get a 'safe' job (whatever that looks like in today's climate, right?). So, you've possibly never considered or been too scared to consider that you can make decisions about your life and decide exactly how it is going to look.

The reason for this is that people like it when we fit into neat little boxes. For example, 'Sarah is a hairdresser, she likes cheap wine and nights out' and 'James is a policeman, he's safe, dependable, quiet and doesn't use social media.' But what happens when Sarah decides to start working towards becoming a lawyer and begins buying fancy wine? What happens when James decides to leave the police force to travel the world and suddenly there are pictures on Instagram of him in Mexico climbing a volcano?

What happens is that the people around them often go into 'freak out' mode. The people they thought they had pigeonholed and knew are no longer following a predictable path and it makes their heads spin. They might then begin criticising, judging and trying to put them back in the box, so that *their* world can once again make sense.

You don't need to make sense to anyone.

You don't have to be the same version of you that you were 10 years ago. You can change your opinion like you change your hairstyle and it's got absolutely nothing to do with anyone else.

Today, you have the choice to decide what your world looks like and to start taking action towards creating this life.

It's time to work out what YOU want

1 **Imagine a life without limits** or barriers and where money is no object. Close your eyes and allow yourself to be childlike and free in your thinking. Think about scenarios from the life you would love to be living. Imagine where you'd live, play out a 'day in the life of' and who you'd be with. I do this type of visualising every night. I don't obsess over how I will make things a reality, I just let my brain take it all in, to play and to show my brain this reality is an option. Try this tonight before you go to sleep.

2 **Write out 30 of the most important 'values' to you.** Imagine these as the ingredients you need to make your life feel great.

They could be things like authenticity, creativity, love, friendship or fun. Let go of judgement while performing this exercise, there is no right or wrong, and these values may change over time. Once you have written the list, narrow it down to your top 10 values and then your top three. Knowing what these are helps us to make better decisions, because we can check that whatever choices we are faced with and decisions we make are aligned with the key values we have and are taking us closer to our 'goal life'.

3 **Make a 'vision board'** (some people call these 'dream boards'). Get your creative hat on and whip up a picture of what you would love your ideal life to look like. Look at houses and holidays, find positive quotes that embody who you want to be and the values you hold. Put this vision somewhere where you can see it regularly and check in with it. It's also lovely to look back on these, to see the progress you've made and how much you have achieved.

"You are always only one choice away from a totally different life."

#16

That thing that happened doesn't define you

'This is Holly, she's a widow.'

We like to put people into groups and to oversimplify to try to make sense of the world around us. We define ourselves and others in broad, sweeping brush strokes, amplifying certain aspects of their or our lives as a way to explain who they or we are.

I *am* a widow but this description of me hardly represents who I am as a woman, it merely conveys a sad fact about something that happened. It would be more truthful to say, 'This is Holly, she's a self-development coach and hides chocolates from her children at the back of the fridge', but this definition of me isn't quite as punchy.

I've never identified with the word 'widow' for this exact reason, although I completely understand why it's helpful for others to use it. It's the same reason we use many other titles: they stop us having to discuss the detail of our pain or explain our current behaviours.

If I were to have a meltdown in the supermarket on Valentine's Day, for example, and were to utter the 'w' word, I'd be scooped up by well-meaning people and showered with love and support. I get the need and the desire to do this but, as with any label, it's rarely reflective of the whole person. What's more, if we aren't careful, these labels can hold us back from being more than just the stuff that has happened.

As you are reading my book, I'm confident that you've had some tough stuff happen in your life. Whether it's that you came from an unsafe home, were bullied at school, have had an awful relationship break-up or someone you love died, you have likely been through something hard.

This chapter is not in any way minimising what has happened. I feel your pain and I have no doubt that you are completely valid in finding it painful. What I want now, though, is for you to find a way to move forwards into your next moment of joy, to acknowledge the pain but to give yourself permission not to camp out there.

You are not what has happened to you.

What's happened is part of the story and we can look for lessons or reflect on what could have been different, but we cannot change the past. Your past might explain why you find certain things challenging in your present, but constantly referring back to it may be keeping you stuck.

When I worked with a client recently, she shared a story of a violent relationship in her past. This was a hellish time for her – deeply frightening and traumatic. She has been working for the past few years on creating a safer and happier life for herself, but the shadow of this period is worn like a cloak around her every day. It shows up in her distrust of others, her fear of stepping out of her comfort zone and her doubt in herself.

Because of this after-effect, she feels the need to refer to what happened almost daily. She believes it explains why she behaves as she does, why she needs such reassurance and lives with a lot of fear. She has shared how awful it feels to talk about it all the time but how she doesn't yet know how to explain who she is now without the old story.

Perhaps this is key, though. At a certain point in your life you were a person who hadn't been through this experience and now you are. Who we are before the crap moments is different to who we are afterwards, and this doesn't mean we are broken or that who we are afterwards is less.

I loved my husband Ross deeply and the pain of his death has changed me completely. I see the world through a different lens and those who meet me at this new stage in my life will be encountering a different person to the one whom Ross knew. Not the fundamentals of me, of course, but I am now a person who has experienced a painful loss and have therefore changed.

Could we, then, begin to reframe our trauma or dark times as moments of transition? A fresh starting point in our lives, where we've learned something new about the world and how we respond to it, and can now begin the next stage.

Steve Taylor PhD published a paper called 'The Transformational Effects of Bereavement' in *Psychology Today* in which he studied the transformational effects and benefits of a bereavement. In his study, participants shared their journeys of finding new values and goals, and of becoming more authentic, self-loving and compassionate following bereavement. Some even felt their experience was akin to a rebirth, such was the impact of the loss.

The stories we tell ourselves about the situation are the reality we will create. We can decide to be defined by our pain or we can decide to alter this way of thinking and become an even better version of ourselves, with a heap more compassion *because* of our painful times.

I'm ready for my transformation...

1 **Notice how you talk about your difficult times**. What does your story sound like and is there a way to frame it so it's easier for you to say and move forward from? When I share my painful story of loss,

I then very quickly share how I feel hope alongside it, and the love I was lucky enough to have experienced with Ross. You may want to consider talking to a professional therapist and getting their help and insight into how you approach your story. I'm a huge advocate of talking therapies as having a space to share with someone outside of your circle can be eye opening and transformative.

2 **Draw a line under the crisis**. Decide that you will be moving forwards now. You might want to mark this transition in some way: a physical change (a dramatic haircut), a move, creating your own transformational ceremony – anything to allow you to feel the shift before you begin walking into the next stage of your life.

3 **Remind yourself that you don't lose the lessons** when you stop giving the trauma all the space in your life. They remain. You do, however, get to feel physically lighter for not carrying the pain into every room.

4 **Choose who you want to be**. If you identify as a label, and perhaps this has even served you up to a point, check in regularly to see if this label is carrying you through this transition or holding you firmly in place. You are not your divorce, your loss or your trauma – you are a fully formed excellent human being.

5 **Write a list of everything you are** outside of the painful stuff. Are you a good friend? Are you a fantastic Irish dancer? Do you cook a knock-out chicken Madras curry or wow people with your napkin-folding skills? Note everything down and see yourself as bigger than one part of your life.

"You are not what has happened to you, you are so much more."

#17

Morning ritual

'Mum, why don't we have a tail?' is an example of the
kind of questions my children tend to ask me first thing in the morning
as I am just beginning to function and open my eyes. Generally, I
respond by picking up my phone to check for any emails or texts I
need to see and then proceed to check my social media, while also
answering the question of the day about our lack of tails or similar.

On my best days, the habit of scrolling first thing won't do me any harm
and I'll probably see something nice like a photo of a friend's baby,
which will make me smile. On a bad day, though, this routine is risky
business. Who knows what you're going to see? Is it your ex and his hot
new girlfriend, a depressing news statistic or the lazy girl from work
celebrating her second promotion in 18 months (while you've been
overlooked *again*). If this second scenario is your morning wake-up then
I guarantee that the next few hours, and possibly even the whole day,
will feel a whole lot harder to deal with than it could have been.

I appreciate that we're all doing our best and I don't want this chapter
to sound like a lecture, with me giving unrealistic 'power morning'
advice that you'll nod your head to, do once and then ignore. I also
can't write about morning routines and pretend that I always get it
right – I would be a total fraud and you'd suss me out in a heartbeat.

What I want to chat about, though, is how we can put in place a really
ace *realistic* morning routine. I'll give you some ideas, then the action
points at the end of this chapter will help you to come up with the
logistics of what this looks like for you. Does that sound all right?

I did a little digging into what the 'successful' folk in the world have been doing with their mornings. Anna Wintour, the editor-in-chief of American *Vogue*, once stated that she wakes at 5 a.m. each morning to play tennis, while Wim 'The Iceman' Hof, a Dutch motivational speaker and extreme athlete, shares his love of ice-cold showers in the morning.

Now, if that's you, then all credit to you. There are some amazing benefits to starting your day early or immersing yourself in cold water. In fact, I actually did a week of ice-cold showers once after reading how they can help your immune system, alertness and resilience, and I really did try to get into them. Unfortunately, I hated every single second, every single time, and couldn't get warm for hours. I know this is because you have to build up tolerance to cold water shock gradually, but it's just not for me. That said, a lovely lady at one of my events told me that she felt the same but wanted the fresh wake-up, so she had a normal-temparture shower followed by an ice-cold face wash. That is now something I do and it feels like a decent happy medium.

My point is that there are ways for us to find the balance between the 'extreme' routines we sometimes hear about and wasting our mornings scrolling, procrastinating and potentially then spiralling into a crappy day. We just have to play around with what works for us.

So, let's look at some popular ideas that are said to create the best mornings:

Set your intention for the day ahead. What is it that you want to focus on? This could be something you need to do or complete or a feeling that you wish to create. Last week, I was in a very 'busy' space with lots of deadlines (real and self-imposed), and I felt rushed and anxious most days. This week, my daily intention is to slow down, focus on one task at a time and to be more mindful. Your intention will be very personal to you. By having one, you know where you are trying to get to.

Meditate. Meditation will always come up in lists of 'good morning rituals' because it's a chance to tune into yourself and where you're at. It's a way to be considered about your day and not to feel the pull to speed to the next job or activity. Now because I like to take the pressure off you, if right now meditation feels too

> **'Your morning is your chance to decide** how you'd like your day to look.'

'grand', start with 10 full breaths and a little 'check-in' with yourself ('Hi Holly, how are you today?').

Drink 'something'. Instagram might suggest you whizz up the perfect green smoothie or some lemon water but I'm just going to tell you to drink 'something' (leave the morning mimosa out though). Get some fluids and some food in your body to fuel and hydrate yourself, and start your day. If you do manage that green drink and hot water and lemon that's lovely, but don't think your morning is doomed if you can't.

Exercise. Whether it's a hardcore weight-lifting session in your home gym, a power walk or jog round the park, or dancing in your underwear over breakfast, try to move your body. If you don't have time to exercise first thing, possibly because you have kids to get ready, at least stretch, flex and be thankful to your body for whichever way it is able to help you through your day.

Get grateful. Yep, gratitude is back and this is an easy win for your morning. List what you feel grateful for to focus your brain. This could be as soon as you wake up or over your morning cuppa, but factoring in gratitude is a fabulous start to any day. For more ideas, *see* 'Gratitude is a game changer' on p. 64.

These are some popular ways people begin their days in a positive fashion, but there isn't an exact science to the perfect morning routine, because we are all different. Creating a routine that works for you, rather than being dragged through your morning in a resistant way, is definitely going to make a difference to your level of 'happy'.

I'm ready to create my routine, where do I begin?

1 Think about it. Consider the ideas we've just chatted about and any you have of your own too. Play around with what feels good to you, experiment and get creative. If after experimenting something doesn't feel right or work for you, don't be afraid to mix it up, take it out and try something else.

2 Make it easy. Creating 'boring' routines can make your life way easier. This means doing things in the same order every day, giving yourself a 'uniform' (if you don't have one to wear already) and eating the same breakfast. The less our brains need to make decisions in the morning the more productive we can be. If you intend to exercise, make sure you've set your alarm and got the childcare sorted if you're heading out, and lay out your sports clothes right next to the bed. Plus go to bed early! For more on this, *see* 'Night-time ritual' on p. 256.

3 Create a 'leave it out' list. Write down the things that aren't making you feel good, that you'd like to leave out of your mornings. Perhaps this could be no social media before a certain time, only chatting to your negative mate after you're fully awake, or leaving the work emails until working hours begin.

4 It's not written in stone. Remember it's OK if you adapt, change or tweak your ideas as you go. It's also OK if some mornings the routine goes out of the window and you find yourself doing everything on your 'leave it out' list. It's never about being hard on yourself and always about being kind to yourself.

#18

It's not all about you

We can all bring to mind the stereotypical image of a spoiled brat. The demanding Veruca Salt who stamps her feet and thinks the world revolves around her, but the truth is that we all sometimes slip into the more subtle manifestation of this behaviour now and again.

Perhaps you think people are talking about you behind your back? Maybe you're scared to do something for fear of judgement? Or is it that you slip into the victim mindset of thinking *your* bad luck is way worse than anyone else's?

No judgement here. This is a judgement-free zone. However, if you tell me that you've never had these moments then I'm going to call BS on that because we have all demanded attention and got caught up in our own story.

We truly are funny little creatures at times, and it would be very easy for any of us to get in our heads and believe that our version of 'difficulty' is worse than that of the people around us. This is our ego speaking. Our ego or egocentric behaviour is about us really focusing in on ourselves and our own view of the world. There are many different but similar definitions of what we mean by ego, but for the sake of argument in this book please assume I mean a preoccupation with self and our own importance.

Now, we can't help this in some ways as we really can only understand the world from our own point of view, but hopefully with practice we can begin recognising that we are part of a wider ecosystem. That how we behave impacts a wider community and that our experiences are no more important than anyone else's.

So why is your ego so unhelpful?

Your ego expects a lot from everyone and everything around you, and those expectations are often very unrealistic. The ego will awaken when you send a text to a friend that gets left unread for a day. The ego will be very angry about this, assuming the friend has ignored you, dismissed you or perhaps even doesn't like you at all!

Your ego will look for happiness outside of you – from people, from status, from stuff – and when that doesn't materialise, it will feel heartily sorry for itself and be pretty grumpy.

Your ego twists your view of yourself and your current reality and may mean you overestimate your abilities and assume you don't have to work all that hard to achieve your goals.

Your ego will insist that when something sad happens in *your* world, the rest of the world should immediately run to your aid, regardless of what's happening in their lives.

Your ego loves praise and accolades and, if left unchecked, will begin craving this stuff, and find it very difficult to achieve happiness when it doesn't have access to it.

Hard fact (and, honestly, I probably will be blunt in this chapter, but know this is a 'love punch' and in no way intended to judge or tear you down, we're all learning here): you're not the only person going through 'it'. Whatever 'it' is, someone else has walked that walk before, someone else is walking 'it' right now and someone else will walk through 'it' in the future.

The unfairness that you are experiencing, or have gone through, is valid and you can absolutely respond accordingly: cry, be mad, make change, take action, whatever you need to do. Unfairness is real life and not a thing only dished out to you. Unfairness isn't equal, though:

some people do seem to get more than their fair share of tough stuff, and avoiding that fact is only going to add to your fury when you feel you've been treated unfairly.

There will be some people who are born into wealth, have beauty, a supportive family and good health, and bounce from success to success.

So what?

Their truth has nothing to do with your own. Another person not being dealt a tough hand has nothing to do with you and your journey, mostly because there is nothing you can do about that. Learning to accept this fact is the first step in setting yourself free.

We put a lot of pressure on ourselves to 'succeed' in life, and when we believe that everything revolves around us it simply piles on the pressure. If the world revolves around you like Jim Carrey's character in *The Truman Show* then all eyes are on what you do. The spotlight is shining brightly at you and every move you make is being observed by others. Even as a confident person this makes me feel a little uneasy.

Try to flip this around: are *you* focused on everyone else around you? Do you go through the conversations of others with a fine tooth comb, pondering the meaning behind it all and endlessly replaying their actions to find fault? I doubt it very much. Our obsession with ourselves being the centre point for everything is nonsense and can really affect our relationships with those around us.

How to keep your ego in check

1 **Shine the spotlight outwards**. When we imagine the world is watching our every move, and that we are the leading character in everyone's lives, it can stop us from being brave, make us fearful of failure and keep us from creating a life we love. When we shine the spotlight outwards on others, we can focus on being of service, of seeing if others are OK. What's more, it can help us consider how we can impact the world, and build our personal confidence as we do so.

2 Ask others about their passions. Ask to see photos of the things that light them up (ask a dog lover about their 'baby' and they will happily gush for hours). There's something wonderful about letting someone talk about what makes them feel good, their special subject, and it's a great lesson in compassion and humility. Take time today to connect with someone and let them talk.

3 Imagine. Take a moment to close your eyes and imagine the whole world on a map. Let your mind wander, zooming into each continent, perhaps swooping into individual countries or cities. Try to imagine different communities, different families, what their individual needs, struggles, wants and desires might be. Notice the similarities between yours and theirs and how everyone is just trying to find their place. As you take your imagined virtual tour, try to notice how unimportant your particular 'challenges' are to those away from you, how focused they are on their own worlds. Then zoom back out, so you can see only the globe. Remind yourself that you are an important part of a bigger picture and that everyone has their role to play. Do this whenever you feel the ego getting loud and remind yourself: *it's not all about you.*

'There will always be someone prettier, wealthier and healthier than you, but so what? Stay in your own lane and focus on your own next steps.'

#19

Negative people, what's their problem?

At the workshops I run I will often ask the group 'How many people here have someone negative in their life?' And every hand shoots up like a rocket, as the energy in the room darkens (and then dissipates into laughter as everyone realises how similar we all are). I imagine as you're reading this you can easily bring to mind one or two people whom you find difficult to be around. In fact, even the thought of these people just made your whole body tense up and want to throw this book against the wall (take a breath, read on first).

In many self-development arenas, the consensus is 'just don't be around negative people' and while that would be lovely, it's unrealistic. Sadly, sometimes the people who infuriate us the most are actually people we also love or *have* to be around. It's simply not always an option to just avoid these people and live in peace. Negative people (in whatever form they take) are here to stay, so we have to learn to navigate around them so we don't lose our minds.

Before we delve in any further, I want us to look at two very important things that we should remember:

1. Everyone is doing the best that they can (even if 'the best that *they* can' doesn't match what you need or want from them).

2. You cannot change anyone else's behaviour – you can only change your own.

Let's be honest though, hearing those two statements is kind of annoying as it's far easier to believe the negative person is an idiot and deliberately making life difficult because they are a bad person. It's also frustrating to realise you cannot learn some special ninja trick to control others and make them behave how you want them to.

When we dislike people's behavior, we zone right into everything bad about them and it's easy to think of people as either 'goodies' or 'baddies'. But we aren't – we are all a mixed bag of positive and negative behaviours and an understanding of this can actually lessen so many of our daily irritations.

Let me give you a great example that a Buddhist meditation teacher once shared with me. This teacher worked every day with a woman who drove her mad because she was difficult, obnoxious and hard to be around. The Buddhist teacher even began dreading going into work. It got so bad that the teacher had zoned into every flaw about this woman, and this woman's ugly shoes became a symbol of what an ugly person she was inside.

Being a Buddhist, however, she knew the work had to come from within herself, so she decided to shift her thinking and compliment this person. The next day at work, she complimented this lady's shoes, telling her she looked lovely in them. In an instant, the 'negative work woman' changed – she lightened, smiled and told the Buddhist teacher that the shoes had been bought on a holiday with her recently deceased mother, and although they were a bit worn they gave her such comfort and held such lovely memories.

From that day onwards, the Buddhist teacher recognised that there is always more than one side to everyone. We are not black and white and everyone is dealing with things we have no clue about. The teacher and co-worker never became best friends, but the encounter helped her to deal with the irritating parts of this woman's personality.

Now let's check out my 'toxic line-up' of negative people and play a game of 'toxic people bingo'. Do you have any of this bunch in your life? And at the bottom of the page we can work out how to deal with them.

- **The Bulldozer** They're emotionally unavailable, thick-skinned, abrupt, with a glass-half-empty and 'I don't care' attitude. They have a sense of self-importance, arrogance and rarely let their guard down in case people use it against them. They only do things that will benefit them and you will never fully feel that close to them.
- **The Drama Queen** Judgemental, envious, critical and dramatic, they spend their time gossiping about others and always have a 'drama' going on in their lives. If they don't have something happening themselves then you bet they will have the latest tale of someone else's misfortune to regale you with over brunch.
- **The Victim** Nothing in The Victim's life is going well (or at least that's how they perceive it) and your time with them will consist of them 'needing to talk' and offloading about the ways they've been hard done by.
- **The Dictator** Controlling, bossy, domineering and manipulative, they are extremely critical of others and believe if people aren't doing things in exactly the way that they would do them, they're fools. The dictator is forceful and will shout people down, not caring how others might feel. As long as they are in charge and things are happening 'their way' then nothing else matters.

How on earth do we deal with negative people?

1 **Create boundaries**. You might not be able to change their behaviour but you can decide what is and what is not acceptable to you. Are you dealing with your own 'stuff' and really can't sit and listen to The Victim's current monologue of woe? Then don't. Not in the mood to hear The Drama Queen's latest hot gossip? Then explain calmly that

you're practising focusing on more positive things, and steer the conversation elsewhere. If people cross your boundaries and won't quit then you have to know that you are allowed to leave. Your life, your rules.

2 **Check in with whether they irritate you because they share traits you think you may have** (or at least worry you might). Sometimes these people can be mirrors that show up our own flaws and that is pretty damn annoying. If this is the case, it's time to do your own inner work.

3 **Remember that they don't think they are negative**, because everyone is doing the best that they can, right? Plus, everyone does things from a belief that what they are doing is the right step to take. That doesn't mean their behaviour is correct, it just means that they are coming from their own place of fear, stress or low self-esteem, and having lived a whole life that you know nothing about. They are navigating life the best way they know how, so you practising empathy, or even pity, can lessen your own distress at their behaviour.

4 **See the lessons**. What is being around these people teaching you? Resilience, patience or perhaps it's making you clarify your own personal boundaries and even learn to stand up for yourself.

5 **Step back**. Sometimes we simply do need to step back from spending time with those who make us feel bad (whatever the reason). Give yourself permission to only see your critical school friend or domineering sibling in short bursts, or when you're emotionally up to it.

'Everyone is doing the best that they can, even if that doesn't match what you need.'

#20

Spilling the tea on fake social media lives

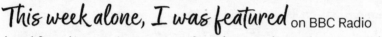 **This week alone, I was featured** on BBC Radio breakfast shows twice, appeared on three podcasts, was quoted in two national newspapers and was nominated for an award.

I have also had a horrendous weekend with my two daughters: sadness about their dad, not wanting to go to sleep and all the normal kids' bickering. I have cried about the fact that I am overwhelmed and out of my depth, had to deal with broken-down appliances and sent my kids to school in unwashed cardigans. Both versions of me are real, but without the knowledge of the latter, the former will trick you into believing my life is polished, glamorous and perfect.

I was introduced to the fakery and glossing-over of perceived imperfections in the media from a young age, and could tell you countless stories of celebrity friends whose online worlds were a far cry from their real lives. But let me share with you my very own experience of trickery...

At 19 (ish, I can't actually remember the exact age), I signed to a record label as a solo singer and was living my life in Newcastle upon Tyne with my parents. I would then commute to London and around the

UK to record, perform and do the rounds of TV, magazine and radio interviews. I spent most of my life on the Newcastle–London King's Cross direct train line, so when *Elle Girl* and *Top of the Pops* magazine (popular teen magazines at the time) asked to do 'A week in the life of...' feature with me, there was a lot of smoke and mirrors' work to be done.

The week prior to my interview with the journalist, the record label paid for me and one member of my music management team to live in an apartment somewhere in London. I brought stuff from home – pictures, posters and things to make it look like I lived there – and got ready to do the interviews.

I was photographed buying flowers in Camden, CDs in a music shop (yep, we still did this then), and at the 'opening' of an art gallery. It all looked very fancy and glamorous. The reality was that I had never bought flowers in Camden in my life, and there was no one in the art gallery with me apart from my team, who promptly shoved a glass of champagne in my hand for the photos to help create the illusion.

The extreme lengths to which influencers and those chasing social media clout are going to is beyond what most of us could possibly imagine. People are faking trips away, taking photos in fake apartments (there is an apartment in Manhattan that can be hired for $15,000 just so people can go there and take photos), or even hiring friends to hang out with them at real or fake events. All this just so they can take photos to induce FOMO (fear of missing out) in their followers, or perhaps show that ex that they're doing just fine without them.

To reveal what was going on, in 2015, an Australian social media 'star' who had amassed more than half a million subscribers on her Instagram account quit the platform. She then changed all the captions on her stunningly beautiful photographs to spell out the reality behind each image. She talked about the endless time it took to take that 'relaxed and caught-off-guard' shot, the loneliness, the starvation, the editing. The pressure this young lady felt is incredibly sad and yet in truth we can all get sucked into the trap of making things look a little better than they really are. For more examples, turn to 'Comparison' on p. 186.

The need to be constantly happy in photos puts such a strain on us. One of my clients recently shared with me four separate 'happy' photos she had uploaded. The truth was she had been genuinely happy in only one of them, and in two she was actively seriously depressed. She hadn't posted them for status or attention, she had just been taught that even when we feel sad we should show ourselves looking happy.

I mean, it really is madness. What does looking at and partaking in this bogus world of social media do to our fragile mental health? By living in this almost augmented reality, where people look like they're one way but are actually the opposite, or at least something different, we are teaching ourselves that we aren't enough and don't have enough. Even when we are enjoying an experience, the constant photo taking and imagining how the video of this will look on social media is driving many of us mad.

People are feeling burned out from trying to work out what's real and what's not, and I for one am craving raw, authentic and honest content. I'd rather hear 'It took me years to build this business. It needed dedication, hard work and consistency' than 'Make a million in 12 months with this secret formula I used to go from broke to buying a Lamborghini.'

Human beings need real connection, and glossy, vacuous, fake living is not it.

How can you protect yourself and not join in the phoney game of 'look at me'?

1 **Challenge yourself to post more 'real' content**. That means no filtering, no editing and sharing the 'other' side of the really lovely photos you took doing that very exciting 'thing' somewhere. Just see what it feels like to go back to the 1990s, when we had one chance at

getting a photo and then had to wait to get it developed, only to discover that lo and behold we had red eye in all the photos and our zip was undone. There was something more honest about that time and, although I'm certainly not saying it was better or worse, I just want to make sure we don't lose ourselves in a blurry filter.

2 **Vote with your feet**. If you follow accounts online that perpetuate the sham 'living my best life' posts, unfollow them in favour of something more nourishing. Perhaps as a collective, if we work together, we can shift the focus. Call it out: we want more 'real'.

3 **Take time out**. Taking time away from social media to pause and reflect on your real world is essential and grounding. If you feel yourself getting sucked down the rabbit hole, it's time to turn off and tune in. Meet a friend in real life, go on a day out with the kids or take a holiday *without* sharing photos of it on social media. I know for many of us this will be hard, but it's a valuable task. There is something fundamentally lovely about keeping part of your world secret and safe within you.

4 **Remember that you don't have to be happy all of the time** and posting photos of you faking happiness will only make you feel worse. Give yourself time to just 'be' and don't feel the need to stay in the rat race of showing up.

'Human beings need real connection, and glossy, vacuous, fake living is not it.'

#21

Tell someone to 'eff off

When you bought this book, perhaps you were under the impression you would be offered some peaceful advice about how to bring more calmness and happiness into your life. Maybe you imagined a monk-like figure with a long beard and wisdom tumbling from his well-travelled spirit. What you've got is a potty-mouthed northern woman who, although I am all about the tranquillity, understands that sometimes in life, in order to create the serene existence you want, you need to pull up your big girl pants and tell someone off.

Feeling angry, or more importantly displaying that anger, can be a shame-filled chasm that many of us desperately try to stay away from and repress. Most of us feel anger in varying degrees at some point or another, and yet we often conceal it and push it far down beneath the surface, fearful that if we express it we'll be shunned.

Of course, there is sometimes a need to do this. As grown adults, we are trying to find the sweet spot that enables us to be direct and clear in our language about what we will accept, while repressing the urge to have a toddler tantrum in the middle of the supermarket because the woman at the checkout won't stop talking and we're late for an appointment.

This is tiring, and can cause a build-up of stress. Imagine a giant bucket. Every time you repress that anger, another drip splashes into the bucket. For a time this will be fine – you'll find happiness outside of the moment that made you angry and you will be able to move forwards. Eventually, though, as each drip lands in your 'anger bucket', the anger is going to spill over.

The trigger often won't be what you think it will be, either. The thing that makes you lose your mind will likely be something innocuous: an off-the-cuff remark from a colleague that lands badly with you, the person who accidentally spills a drink on to your gorgeous new outfit or the idiot who cuts you up on your commute to work. Something will happen that will unleash all manner of hell on to the perpetrator and leave you feeling out of control.

This is not the kind of empowering anger we want. This untamed explosion won't result in you walking away with a swagger, feeling proud for sticking up for yourself. Instead, it will leave you feeling ashamed and embarrassed. The opposite situation is no good either: if you constantly curb your fury and don't feel able to speak your mind at all, then you could end up being taken advantage of.

Finding the balance between the two is my focus for us here. I want you to know that on the one hand you can rise above the BS and choose your battles wisely, but on the other hand you can tap into your inner lion and hold your own when the situation calls for it. By this, I mean that you show your anger at a situation without exploding into rage.

If you are naturally more submissive, you need to learn to not let people bulldoze past your boundaries and push you around. You don't need to become a whole different person to do that. Being quietly confident and strong is all that is needed, and will be a far more effective way of getting the outcome that you want than being loud and obnoxious.

One day, you are going to find yourself in a position in which someone hasn't played fairly – they've done something that is completely unacceptable to you and they couldn't care less about your feelings. On one of these occasions you are going to stand up tall, puff out your chest and tell that person to "eff off!' in words that may or may not be more eloquent. You're then going to walk away feeling like a 'boss' and know that standing up for yourself is a powerful confidence-booster and much better than exploding into rage.

When I was younger, I was a real people pleaser. I hated the idea that I might offend and was always allowing people to walk all over me. I remember the feeling the day I found my voice. I was working on an acting job for a low-budget, small film. I was doing a favour for a friend and was told my travel would be paid for and I would be provided with food on the day. I was already an established actress and was bringing some credibility to the film. They knew this and I knew this, although I wouldn't dream of being the person who pointed this out. And yet after filming had finished, I wasn't paid for my travel. It was around £60 and I knew they had clearly spent their budget and were trying to get out of paying me. Old me would have dropped it, swallowed the loss and kept my anger inside, but this was a new me and I decided that I was not going to accept it.

'Stand tall, puff out your chest and know there is no better feeling than speaking your honest, unfiltered truth.'

I felt sick to the stomach making the phone call to confront the producer. All of the reasons why I should just leave it were swirling around my head but I knew that if I didn't do this now I would be forever accepting this kind of crap.

I made the call (with the notes in front of me that I had written in case I wobbled). I focused on calm breathing and I told the producer how annoyed I was and how disrespectful his behaviour had been. I demanded my money and informed him that I would be taking my complaint to the actors' union Equity if he didn't fulfil our contract. He paid up and apologised profusely. The rest of the actors got paid too, and I felt elated.

In life, there are times when you have to dramatically walk out of a job, break up with a partner, sever a friendship and raise your voice to be heard. Do all of these things sparingly and with thought, but know that when required you can evoke your inner sass and won't be spoken down to.

How to speak your mind and still be kind

1 Keep calm. Take a big breath, relax your shoulders, say what you need to say and let go of the outcome. Don't allow yourself to be frazzled and browbeaten by anyone, don't allow yourself to be sucked into a petty back-and-forth and throwing-down of childish accusations. You decide how this is going to go.

2 Use affirmations. Before a confrontation of any kind, saying one of these statements out loud to yourself as a mantra can be a great way to stay on track and calm under pressure. Whichever statement you choose, say it at least five times, while breathing calmly:

- 'I am calm and considered.'
- 'I make my points clearly.'
- 'My points are valid.'
- 'I deserve to be heard.'
- 'I am calm under pressure.'

For more, check out 'Affirmations' on p. 104.

3 Practice makes perfect. Practise difficult conversations before you have them, including ones during which you suspect you'll have to raise your voice and get angry. Practise the moment you might tell someone to 'get lost' or 'to go to hell!' and desensitise yourself to the words and how it feels to say them.

4 Remember that the person may not even be aware that they have upset you or that you feel intimidated, sidelined or attacked by them. They may have no clue they just stepped across one of your boundaries. It's your job to educate them. The next time someone pushes their luck with you, set the fire free and tell them in no uncertain terms, 'Absolutely not!' Whatever happens next will unfold as it does, but there is no better feeling than speaking your honest, unfiltered truth.

#22

Nature not Netflix

The WhatsApp group is pinging away, I've got a text message (sadly, probably from Domino's Pizza rather than one of my actual friends), the emails are mounting up, and my social media has hundreds of notifications. I hear my children chatting to their friends on FaceTime and I watch a YouTube video as I make my morning cup of tea. It's only a few minutes into my day and there is often so much noise I can hardly concentrate.

I love technology, don't get me wrong, and I am the first to enjoy binge-watching a series on Netflix and connecting with people online. But if the balance of technology and nature becomes swayed too far towards the tech, I know that I'm going to begin to feel dreadful.

Scientists believe that our brains weren't cut out to have so much stimulation all of the time. This is backed up by the fact that we have seen an increase in burnout and overwhelm since the birth of the internet.

Growing up in Newcastle, a busy city, I have a vivid memory of a conversation with my dad about lifestyle. He was looking wistfully out of our sitting room window and said, 'I want more than looking out of this window and just seeing another row of houses. I want greenery, nature, something real.'

I was 16 and all I was excited about was being able to go clubbing in a few years and being with my friends. I looked at my dad like he was an alien and shrugged off this remark as 'an old man' comment (scarily, my dad was not far off my current age during this conversation).

I now understand completely why he had this pull towards the great outdoors and I share the same wisdom with my daughters when I drag them off their iPads and make them 'hug a tree' in the park (and yes, this is literally what I make them do, I am that Mum).

We are part of nature.

Fresh air, green trees and a sea breeze do something to our psyche and re-energise us in a way that we don't get while purchasing iPhone chargers on Amazon (seriously, where do all the iPhone chargers in my house go?). Whether you're a city lover or a country gal we all need 'more green and less screen'. And if you have any doubts, know that apart from our own anecdotal experiences of 'it's lovely to get out in the fresh air' there are actual scientific studies to back up what we instinctively know.

For instance, a study in Japan during which participants were asked to walk in built-up urban areas or in lush green forests showed that the forest walkers recorded significantly lower heart rate and blood pressure levels than their urban counterparts. In fact, less stress has been reported after just 20 minutes of walking in green spaces, and being outdoors can help restore our focus and support us in being more creative and giving us more vitality. All in all, the research states that being in nature is a very valuable way to help us feel a little more blissful in our minds and hearts.

You may also be wondering if my dad ever got to live out his dream of less concrete and more hills. I am happy to report that he did. He now lives in a place surrounded by mother nature and is thrilled to bits with this transition.

Get me to the garden, I want to feel great!

1 **Listen to the sounds of nature**. There are plenty of playlists online that will instantly transport you to a beach or rainforest. In terms of impact on our mental health, studies have shown that just listening to these intoxicating natural sounds can help calm our fight-or-flight response and relax our nervous system. So, crank up the thunderstorms or trickling waterfall sounds and bask in your very own tropical paradise.

2 **Draw**. Go for a walk and collect some leaves, acorns, sticks or rocks, bring them home and draw them. Getting arty with nature is very therapeutic and shouldn't only be the pastime of children (although they will love it, too). Plus, you really don't have to be any good at it to experience the benefits; it's about your focus and joy, not trying to be the next big nature artist on the block.

3 **Become a tourist**. There are likely to be many places in your local area that you have yet to explore. It's easy to take ourselves somewhere else when we want to find solace and calm, but very often there are splendid places locally. Stick on the walking boots and go and find some undiscovered gem that is right under your nose. Perhaps you could even take along a little picnic with you, too...

4 **Enjoy the sunset**. Sunsets may be my favourite thing ever. I am a 'sky nerd' and the colours and vastness of them just instantly make me happy. I see it as the universe giving me a free gift (and I know this has slipped me into the 'hippy dippy' bracket, but that's the kind of glee I am going to spout when there's a sunset in my view). Find out the time at which the sun will set near you and head to a local nature spot to watch the day turn to night (I promise it'll be worth it).

5 **Do a scavenger hunt**. There are loads of pre-prepared ones on Pinterest but it really doesn't need to be too fancy. Write down 20 things to spot while out in nature and then take yourself off on a walk to find them. There's something mindful and lovely about really looking as you step out into the wild world and it can be fun to bring in this element of play to your walks.

'We *are* nature, so get outside to connect with yourself.'

#23

Affirmations

When you say 'affirmations' in the world of self-development it often lands in people's ears in one of two ways. The first is 'I haven't a clue what you're talking about, Holly.' And the second is that the listener imagines me emerging draped in white linen, covered in 'meaningful' tattoos from Bali and talking about my 'feminine powers'.

So let me break down for you what affirmations really are, while shattering some misconceptions and stereotypes as we go.

Affirmations (or 'mantras' as some people call them) are positive sentences said in the present tense. They are intended to train your brain to focus on certain areas of your life, and to challenge any negative thoughts. For example, if you are looking to find a new job you might say, 'I see opportunities everywhere', or when I'm in a hurry and my daughters are taking an *unbelievable* amount of time to get dressed, I may say, 'I have time for this' so I don't lose my mind. The job of an affirmation is to 'affirm' to your brain the things that you want to be true, to teach your brain to be open to the possibility of making them so, and ultimately to encourage you to take action towards making them a reality.

There's nothing too fancy about affirmations, and honestly that's one of the reasons I like to use them. They provide an easy win and are something anyone can do. You can say them out loud or write them down; either way, repetition is key.

And yet affirmations can be contentious because some people simply use them in the wrong way. For example, if a person shouts 'money comes easily to me' in their bedroom and nothing happens immediately, they may end up feeling frustrated and wondering why they aren't a millionaire. But this is not how affirmations work.

Affirmations aren't magic; it's not some 'hocus pocus' wishful thinking. Affirmations can only work if you get your subconscious on board, too (i.e. if you truly embody the belief), and are therefore encouraged to take action to achieve it. If, in this money example, the person shouts 'money comes easily to me' but in her subconscious she believes money is really hard to come by, then the conflict between the old subconscious belief and the affirmation is going to be too big a leap. The person won't take any action and therefore won't make any money.

With affirmations, you often have to work up to believing them, so the best way of doing this can be to make your affirmations feel transitional or that you're working towards something. That way, your subconscious won't have a toddler tantrum and sabotage your efforts. Here's an example from my own life to explain how it can work.

As I grew up on TV and had make-up artists 'correcting' my face every day as a teenager, it's no wonder I began to get some body image issues. I say that lightly, but in reality I truly thought I was revolting and hid my face and body behind mountains of fake tan and make-up.

If during that time in my life I had been told by some well-meaning self-help 'guru' to affirm 'I am beautiful' while standing naked in front of a mirror, I would have rolled my eyes so hard I'd have sprained them. Saying 'I am beautiful' at that moment would have been too great a leap for me and my subconscious would have stamped its feet like a three-year-old. I'd have received no benefit from doing that affirmation at that time and so I had to start small and work my way up.

So, I used the phrase 'I am OK.' It may seem like a sad little affirmation but it was way better than the other stuff I was saying in my head at that time. I then moved on to 'I look nice sometimes' and *eventually* 'I am beautiful' – but not overnight (and not naked in my mirror … probably).

By doing affirmations this way I was able to softly coax my subconscious into getting on board and creating a new pathway in my brain.

As with everything I love about the route to feeling good, it's about simplifying the methods and finding what works for you.

Is there any science behind affirmations then? I am happy to report that there is. There have been many studies into whether or not affirming statements work, most notably the Steele CM 1988 study. This came to the conclusion that when people choose to self-affirm they do see a positive impact on how they deal with everyday threats and difficulties, and thus affirmations can be used as a very valuable tool in our 'let's get happy' arsenal.

The reason affirmations seem to work is twofold: first, we like talking and affirming what is valuable to us and, second, when we feel under threat and like we have failed or been criticised in some way, affirmations can be used to top up our feelings of self-worth.

Essentially, repeating affirmations helps to train your brain that the words you are saying are what you want it to create as a reality (see 'How the brain works' on p. 16 to remind yourself how the RAS funtions). Affirmations, when fully embodied, give us the encouragement we need to take action to achieve them.

Every time I do a speaking event at which there might be hundreds or even thousands of people I say, 'I enjoy meeting new people' or 'I tell my story with ease', which helps me to make this concrete in my mind. You too can use affirmations in any area of your life and watch them help you step into your best self.

'I am brave and resilient and it's my time to shine.'

I'm down for these affirmations, where do I start?

1 **Pick any area of your life you want to focus on** and write down 10 affirmations that relate to it in a positive way. The shorter and sharper the better, and always put the affirmation in the present tense as if it is already happening: 'I am confident and strong'; 'I am enough'; 'Good things are happening'. I like to choose one or two affirmations to focus on per day.

2 **Commit to a time to work on your affirmations**. You could set a reminder on your phone so alerts come up at various points throughout the day. Alternatively, link your affirmation work to particular events in your day – perhaps you do them in the car, in the shower or as you cradle your morning coffee. Setting these times will remind you to practise your affirmations and help train your brain to think in the way you want it to.

3 **Say these affirmations out loud at least five times**. Don't just say them in your head, speak them out loud.

4 **Write them down** on sticky notes or on a white board. I'm a big fan of the white board as this means I can write out my daily mantras and notes for myself the night before and see them in the morning as I wake.

5 **Lend spice to these affirmations** by adding in a gesture to go with them. Yes, I know you're already cringing at the thought of what this might look like, but I'm not asking you to make this something you do in weekly board meetings, just in the comfort of your own private space. It could be as simple as saying, 'I am loved' and placing your hands on your heart.

#24

What they think is none of your business

I consider myself, for the most part, a person who doesn't make decisions based on what other people think about me. I have high self-esteem and I know who I am, but even with all of that, if I really think about it, I make hundreds of micro decisions every day that are based on what others will think about me.

I woke up today and chose an outfit knowing I was walking my daughters to school and that later that day I would be at a meeting at a hotel. I therefore chose not to wear joggers and trainers and spent a little more time doing my hair – a decision that was (whether I like to admit it or not) based on the fact that I would be seeing other people.

I'm OK with this fact. We are a social species with a desire to fit in and survive, so a low-level amount of concern for what others think causes us very little issue. However, for some of us, we can find ourselves becoming fixated on what others may say about us and trapped in a vicious cycle of approval addiction. This can leave us bouncing between worry, anxiety, neediness and insecurity before every decision.

I am asked to be a guest speaker at many events and conferences and as I stand on those stages and share my journey or knowledge, every single person watching me has a different opinion. Some will think I'm a great speaker and love the outfit I have chosen, some will think my northern accent is irritating and that my dress sense is tacky. Both of those opinions are valid. Neither of those opinions has anything to do with me.

When any of us forms an opinion we base it on our own judgements, past expectations, likes, dislikes and fears. We have all experienced different things in our lives and formed our unique perspective of the world. This means that two people can witness exactly the same thing and see it completely differently, and those two people can be around you and view you completely differently too.

Not everyone is going to like you.
Not everyone is going to 'get' you.
Not everyone is going to think you're amazing at what you do.

Some people are idiots.
Some people offer their opinion when it is not asked for.
Some people will always have something negative to say.

On the other hand...

You do not like everyone.
You do not 'get' everyone.
You do not think everyone is good at what they do.

You are sometimes an idiot.
You sometimes give your opinion when it is not asked for.
You sometimes say negative stuff for no reason.

Welcome to being a human being.

We must learn to recognise that we have the power to choose whether we allow someone else's opinion of us to become our identity or whether we use my favourite phrase when someone imparts their summary of who they think I am: 'Hmm, that's interesting.'

Using that little sentence allows me to become an investigator and to take a moment to consider what is being said. It enables me to distance myself from the words being used and to work out whether there is anything for me to learn or whether this is something to ignore.

Essentially, we have to listen to where the message is coming from. Is this a person whom you would go to for advice? Is this a person who has a particular knowledge in the area they are critiquing? Is this advice constructive and helpful? If it ticks these boxes then perhaps there is some work to be done on your part, a little tweak here and there, or perhaps you've even completely messed up (and this is OK too!). If when you check in it meets none of these criteria then you should remind yourself that what is being said is only one view of you and truly isn't factual.

> **'Live your life like no one is paying attention to what you do, because they're not.'**

When we get caught up in worrying about other people's opinions of us it can keep us stuck. You don't always need approval and, if you train yourself to believe in you and be your own best cheerleader, then that desire to seek validation from others will diminish rapidly.

My husband Ross, who had autistic spectrum disorder (ASD) and thus was extremely honest and spoke his mind (as he saw it), would often find himself on the receiving end of someone being offended by his words. He would say regularly, 'They have allowed themselves to be offended.' For some reading this, your instant reaction would be 'No, *you* have offended me, *you* have made me angry' and although I understand why you have come to this conclusion, learning to own your reactions and responses to any given situation is key.

You felt angry or offended or sad or inspired because of the meaning you have put on what has happened. Equally, others can be offended by your actions, but this is again based on their model of the world and has truly nothing to do with you.

Of course, there are times when how you act does have consequences – I'm not talking about breaking the law or official codes of conduct here, or about upsetting everyone in your workplace or family by deliberately going out of your way to be obnoxious. I mean that in a general sense we should worry less about what people think. So, although you will never be able to avoid caring about other people's opinions completely, let's now look at ways you can care a little less.

I don't want to let other's opinions control my life, what shall I do?

1 **Get to know yourself**: your values, likes, dislikes and fears. The more you know who you are, the less likely it is that your self-esteem will crumble the moment someone questions you.

2 **Mind your own business**. More often than not, someone's opinion of you is their business. The fact that Chrissie from work has a bad attitude is her business. The fact that your mum is never on time for your brunch dates – her business. What is *your* business is how you respond to, interpret and work through all of life's challenges. Stay in your own damn lane.

3 **They don't care**. No one cares as much about you and your life as you. No one is looking at your mistakes with a magnifying glass or mulling over whether you are a 'good enough' human. Think about it: do you really analyse other people in the way you assume they are doing to you? Of course not, and imagining that they are giving you this time is putting undue pressure on yourself (and is fairly egocentric!). For more on this, *see* 'How to keep your ego in check' on p. 86.

4 **Mess up, it's OK**. Making a fool of yourself is really not the worst thing in the world. Failing, while it might sting, is an important part of life and you do not need to be perfect (in fact it's a pretty impossibly tall order). Think about what the worst-case scenario really is (you brought that to mind really quickly, didn't you?), and then play it out to its full conclusion. I imagine you will notice how extreme this version is. Remind yourself that whatever happens (which is really unlikely to be the extreme version you just imagined), you will deal with it, like you have dealt with everything up to this point already.

#25

Whatever gets you through the tough bits

I spoke to a woman recently who spent the first year after her husband's death wearing his clothes and aftershave, and sleeping on his side of the bed in an attempt to feel close to him. What we do to get through our moments of difficulty is individual, honest and important. We shouldn't dismiss our needs during these challenging times or minimise the importance of our rituals.

I can write endlessly about tips and ideas that may help you cope, but ultimately it's about finding what works for us individually and leaning into these practices when needed. I find that people often apologise for their behaviour and assume their wacky way of getting through their hard moments makes them bizarre. It doesn't, it makes you human. Your brain is doing its very best to work its way through trauma and to survive.

Your brain is a survivor. YOU are a survivor and your inventive mind is going to search for and create all kinds of new and innovative ways to cope with these tough times. You might find yourself doing things that you have never done before and adopting new, unconventional strategies to get yourself motivated and out of bed. As long as you aren't harming yourself or putting others in danger then the off-the-wall and peculiar new habits are completely and utterly fine.

I am a doer during times of trauma or difficulty. I like to stay active and productive. I like to have a goal I am working towards and usually the end goal will mean being able to help others in some way too. Many will look at my behaviour during my well-documented 'crappy times' and, based on their model of the world, think I should slow down. That's OK, because it's not their thing to cope with.

Maybe you're a doer? Perhaps after that relationship break-up you suddenly had the urge to redecorate the entire house. Obsessing over each room and creating endless Pinterest boards of inspiration. Or after the death of your sibling, did you find yourself on a mission to raise money for your child's school's sports equipment fund? Working towards a goal can help to focus the mind away from the pain.

A friend of mine, Jess Mckee, enrolled herself in a sports pageant after the death of both of her parents and found herself on stage in front of hundreds of people. She also relocated from her home town and ran the London Marathon. During all of this she was grieving, living with trauma and working through her pain. Was she 'fine' throughout it all? No. Did she cry? Lots. Alongside the tough stuff though, the things she got herself involved in contributed to her healing.

When I asked on my Instagram account about the ways my followers dealt with their pain, it was varied, amusing, wonderful and so very similar. Host of *The Waffle Shop* podcast, Taylor James, a mental health campaigner, shared his own unique way to de-stress: watching chiropractor videos on YouTube. I wasn't aware this was even a 'thing', but it is and if it helps then that's just great.

None of these examples may be what you believe 'trauma' looks or behaves like, but all of them are valid and perfectly great ways of walking through stuff.

You may be reading this and thinking, 'I can't think of anything worse!' Perhaps for you, the idea of 'doing' when you feel rubbish is the opposite of what you need. Maybe you need to retreat, be silent and reflect. I have friends who turn to God or religion of some kind, and others who write or draw. I know people whom I won't hear from at all while they work out their 'new normal' and I understand we all process differently.

There are also those of us who find ourselves seeking to distance ourselves from the site of the trauma a little (or a lot). Perhaps the tough times make you move house, quit your job, emigrate to a different country or travel the world.

Whatever you do, these are all coping strategies. They are all valid and the likelihood is that you will find yourself going through a mix of them all at different points on your journey. It's important that you consciously become aware of what you need and listen to your body, mind and heart.

It's so strange to me how much judgement is associated with how we get through things. We look in on other people's worlds, observing them and comparing their choices to how we might get through the same situation (*see also* 'Comparison' on p. 186). It's human nature, of course, yet it's incredibly unhelpful to those in the thick of their difficulties.

Let us try to be open-minded to all paths and send love to those going through stuff. Some go to the gym, some have lots of sex, some decide to live on a boat and 'Eat, pray, love' their way forwards. Let yourself and them off the hook because none of us really has any idea how we will react given the same set of circumstances.

When things get rough, how to get tough...

1 **Be your own BFF**. Just like you would with a friend, ask yourself what you need and see what your unconscious mind brings up for you. I mean literally ask, whether that's in your head or out loud, 'Holly, what do you need?' and then listen to your gut and don't overthink

the answer. If you ask and today you need to cry in a ball on the floor, honour the feeling and act accordingly. If today you need to sign up to run a marathon for charity, then take action and go for it.

2 **Let go of judgement about your choices**. There is no right or wrong here. You can't ace or fail getting through difficult times. This isn't about winning or losing, it's about surviving and helping yourself to thrive (even on the days when you're not feeling very 'thrive-y').

3 **Drop the labels**. As we walk through these hurdles, we can be very critical of ourselves and it hinders our progress. You're not one thing, you're not broken, you're just a person going through and navigating a difficult situation.

4 **Notice and become aware of any judgement** you are currently holding about others and how they 'should' be dealing with their life hardships. Challenge any of these thoughts as they arise and remind yourself that we are all just trying to find our path and just because someone else's is different to yours, it doesn't make it wrong.

"There's no acing or failing the tough times, just do what works for you to thrive and survive."

#26

Addicted to drama

'No more drama in my life' may have been something you've blurted out before as you channel your inner Mary J. Blige during a particularly stressful time. I know I've said it and I know I've meant it. However, if I'm honest, there are times when I have proclaimed to want to avoid drama while actively courting it.

We, as human beings, are addicted to drama, by which I mean a state of negative excitement (with all its angst). The thrill of hearing a fresh piece of gossip or the giddy feeling of being the first to tell someone something you're not supposed to know can be intoxicating.

We have access to drama in many areas of life. Newspapers sell us the latest political drama, celebrity gossip magazines keep us in a frenzy with Hollywood scandals, and our neighbours, family and friends keep us up to date with the personal lives and secrets of those closest to us. Each touch point pumps into our brains and feeds our need for more.

The problem is that we can get addicted to drama without even realising it and then it's very hard to get out of the habit of consuming it. I bet that before reading this chapter you hadn't even considered how much 'drama' was already around you, and being in this state certainly doesn't create a space in which to thrive.

Perhaps you're reading this after having just spent an hour scrolling through a Facebook spat or having binged on reality TV and are now wondering if you're a drama junkie? Let me help you out with some questions to ask yourself:

- Are you always in everyone else's business?
- Do you start conversations with 'You're not going to believe this!' or 'Have you seen what's been going on with…?'
- Do you watch lots of reality TV or high-drama programmes?
- Do you post attention-seeking social media posts and then check to see if anyone has commented every second breath?
- Do you always have a 'thing'? A health complaint, job loss, dating disaster, a death or a 'crisis' and does it feel like you wouldn't know what to do if everything was going great?
- Do you lean towards overreacting to things and overthinking them?
- Are you a moaner?
- Have others around you muttered, 'Wow you just have no luck' or something to that effect after being regaled with another climatic episode of your roller-coaster life?

If you mentally just nodded along to each bullet point and possibly even gave a little gasp as you noticed just how many you do (because a gasp adds a little dramatic effect, right?) then we have some work to do.

Being in this high-chaos cycle with adrenalin coursing through your veins cannot remain your constant state or you'll eventually crash from exhaustion (and then complain about all the drama that just falls into your lap).

I will fully admit that I noticed elements of drama addiction in myself. Having been on the acting merry-go-round for so long, I'd got used to the highs and lows, the need to strive and bounce back, so it's easy to see how living in this heightened state could become habitual. When I made the decision to remove the drama from my life I initially found the silence without it deafening.

For, in truth, the fast-paced nature of drama can also be a lovely distraction from having to take real action, especially if it's not really your personal drama you're indulging in. The impact of the silence you experience when you remove the drama can be that you start to see the world as a more negative and lonely place, which initially sees your levels of happiness lower. So how on earth do we stop?

The first step in lessening the drama is to notice where it is coming from and where you can begin distancing yourself from it. This doesn't mean you can never indulge in a lunchtime gossip with your mates, but it does mean that you might need to step back from it for now, until you feel confident it's not the only type of conversation you're having. When you are your happiest self you may be fine catching the news or watching some dramatic crime documentary, but when life is already stretching you it's worth noticing where you have the control to allow something into your space or not.

Begin to redirect your energy into more joyful and positive activities. Perhaps you could get that energy 'high' from taking up a sport or engaging in some thrill-seeking physical activity. Take away the drama 'craves' by climbing a mountain or surfing the waves. Find time to be around others who engage in positive talk and know that training your brain to stop chasing drama is the fastest route to peace and happiness.

I'm exhausted and I want calm. What shall I do?

1 **Mind your own damn business**. I know this is brutal, but begin to consider whether this is something you 'need' to get involved in. Will getting involved bring peace into your life or send you spiralling into turmoil that you could do without?

2 **Do a drama detox**. Get out a pen and paper and write down all the areas of your life that bring in high-intensity drama, struggle or crisis (and this includes the people who bring it, too). Noticing where things are coming from is an important step and you may be surprised what comes up. I recently found myself becoming addicted to having political rows with people on Twitter (we all have to have a hobby, right?), and then had to delete the app until I got a grip on the need to feed the drama.

3 **Go cold turkey**. Just like any addiction, there comes a point when you have to abstain altogether, to lessen the grip the addiction has on you. It is said that it takes 21 days to break a habit, so my challenge to you is to go 21 days without gossip, without dramatic TV and without the news (whichever areas you find you're drawn into most, or all of them if you're ready to rip the bandage off).

4 **Be still**. Oh stillness and quiet, the arch enemy of the drama queen. This may be your biggest challenge, but learning to be still, to be silent, to take lovely full breaths and notice the excitement in the mundane (a paradox I know, but work with me) will help you to live in a space of tranquillity you might not previously have found.

5 **Listen**. I challenge you today to find your fave spot in your home or outside, sit there and either listen to music or just the general noises around you. Leave your phone somewhere you can't grab it and give yourself the gift of calm.

'Training your brain to stop chasing drama is the fastest route to peace and happiness.'

#27

Watch your mouth

This chapter is all about bad language. For anyone who follows me on social media, has been to an event I've run or even stood within one metre of me, you might be thinking this is somewhat ironic because I swear in a way that would make sailors wince. But this isn't the type of 'bad language' we will be discussing here.

What I am referring to is words with negative connotations and angry words – words that have an instant impact on our minds when we hear them. The frustrating thing with some of this negative language is that we have become so habitual in our use of it that we no longer recognise it as negative, and so without even realising it, we are impacting our mood with our words.

The science to back this up is pretty compelling and there have been various studies done on the impact of language on our brain. One important study was undertaken by Maria Richter and her team from the Department of Neurology at Friedrich Schiller University Jena in Germany. In it, they showed that when subjects were confronted with negative words, both imagined and said out loud, the brain responded by releasing stress hormones into the body, proving that words really can affect us on a deep psychological level.

Dr Andrew Newberg (a neuroscientist) and Mark Robert Waldman (a communications expert) agree, and wrote a book called *Words Can Change Your Brain: 12 Conversations to Build Trust, Resolve Conflict, and Increase Intimacy* (Penguin, 2014) in which they concluded that not only do negative words make our bodies produce stress hormones, but using positive language can change your reality for the better.

I love words. I'm a word nerd and so this subject has always fascinated me. I'm also obsessed with finding tiny daily tweaks that can really shift whether we feel happy or not, and so the idea that if you change your words you can begin changing how you feel is very exciting for me, and hopefully for you too!

Let's have a look at things we might say every day and consider how they may alter the way we experience our lives:

'Hi, how are you?'

'*Not* bad.'

This is my favourite example of a daily dose of negative language. How often have you said the words 'not bad' and had no knowledge of what that message is telling your brain? You see, your brain can't tell the difference between real and imagined and it's constantly on the look-out for 'threats' to your well-being. So your brain fails to notice the word 'not' and accepts the word 'bad' as reflecting how you feel. You may think you are innocently rounding up the feeling of just an average day, but your brain was just given the indication that things aren't good.

Now before you spin out and become a self-elected mute, fearful of the words coming out of your mouth, this is not a 'once it's said, you're going to instantly start to feel rubbish' kind of gig. It is just something we can begin to watch in ourselves and self-correct accordingly. It's so easy to slip into these patterns of talking because everyone else is doing it, too, but you aren't just anyone, you are a person who is aiming to feel more happy and less crappy and you are going to be a change-maker and lead the way.

Let's look at some other descriptive words and sentences that might come up:

- 'It's a nightmare!'
- 'It's disastrous!'
- 'I'm furious they're backing us into a corner!'
- 'I'm distraught I've lost my job.'
- 'We have a problem.'

Just reading that list to myself instantly shifted my emotional state. If someone describes something as 'a nightmare' to me, my imagination goes to the darkest depths of human experience. In truth, though, this particular 'nightmare' may refer to the fact that you've lost the expensive glasses that you bought only last month. Similarly, hearing the word 'problem' causes a fixed and stuck feeling within many of us, whereas if we were to describe it as a 'challenge' then the threat level our brain perceives is very different. We can 'rise to a challenge' – it feels like something we can walk ourselves through.

The words you choose to use – and there are currently (according to the second edition of the Oxford English dictionary) around 600,000 of them in English – will create the frame you put around all that you experience.

When I had to come home to my two young daughters and tell them that their lovely daddy had died, and watch them sob unconsolably in my arms as I felt my heart breaking, I would have been forgiven for describing that moment as a 'nightmare'. And indeed other people did decribe what I was going through as this, but I chose different words. I chose different words not to minimise the pain or to avoid what was happening but because I knew choosing better words would reframe what I was living through and, quite honestly, what I was living through and trying to get my girls through was tough enough without making it even worse.

Instead, when people asked me how I was during that time, I didn't lie and say, 'Well I'm just wonderful, my fine friend and how are you?'

(toxic and fake positivity is not what this is about). Instead, I would say, 'I'm OK, I'm working through things and I will be all right.' Using those more positive words gave me hope, reminded me I would be OK and helped me enormously.

Now it's your turn

1 **Notice the negative words and phrases you habitually use**. Notice the words those around you use and seek out better alternatives. 'No problem' could be 'sure, of course' or 'I'm devastated' could be 'I'm disappointed'. See how lowering the intensity of the language starts to feel for you and how quick you get at self-correction.

2 **Write down as many positive words as you can think of**, such as love, excitement, wonder, joy, pleasant and wonderful, and seek to add to that list. Aim to use as many positive words in your day as possible.

3 **Remember that you have the power to choose**, you decide the stories you tell yourself. Now you know the strength of using transformational vocabulary you can find ways to bring more positivity into your life.

'Your words have power, use them wisely.'

#28

Ask for help

As a staunchly independent woman (insert Beyoncé-style hand gesture and hair flick) I have often struggled to ask for help. I want to be self-sufficient and strong, and to know that if I were left in the woods with nothing but myself I would survive (and in my mind probably be able to fight off a bear!).

I don't know about you, but I think that over the years I have concocted a story that asking for help is a bit shameful and somehow implies I have failed or 'can't cope'. That the moment I utter the words 'I need some help' the music will be turned off abruptly and everyone will turn to stare at me (perhaps a few will even shake their heads slowly). This is a very vivid image from my brain that has kept me fearful of allowing people to help.

I say 'allowing' because I do believe largely that people want to help. I believe in people, I think most are pretty decent and sometimes, especially when it's clear we are going through some stuff, our friends and loved ones feel completely unable to help and desperately want to.

It was in fact my husband, Ross, who began to teach me to reframe my story that asking for help was weak. When he was told he would have back-to-back radiotherapy for a month, we knew that this would mean we had to drive 40 minutes from our home to the hospital every day. With two kids at school and nursery this would have been a challenge, and although I wanted to be there with Ross every step of the way, logically I knew it was unnecessary. Ross enlightened me during that time by reminding me that people wanted to help, and that by scheduling in friends and family, allocating them a day to take him to the hospital, we would actually be giving them a gift.

I hadn't thought about asking for help in this way before, but then I flipped it around and imagined how I would feel if one of my friends was going through what we were, and how I'd be chomping at the bit to be given a job to do that would ease their pain. It suddenly made perfect sense and since then I have used this logic to help me fight against my instant urge to retreat and be the one who can 'do it all'.

That's just it though, isn't it? We can't 'do it all' and we really don't have to. There are going to be times in your life when you need help, when it's all become too much and you need reinforcements. It might not even be your breaking-point moments, it may just be that you don't have a particular skill and taking the time to learn this skill, just to prove you can, is a waste of your time and energy.

As a petite woman, I have in the past found myself lugging large items around just to prove I can, and making my life much harder than it needed to be. However, in the last few years I have challenged myself to reach out to people and ask for help. Rather than breaking my neck to get a chest of drawers up the stairs I have waited and asked for the support of some of the men in my life. Do they then judge me for asking? No. They are thrilled to help and glad they don't have to think about me struggling.

Asking for help is an act of bravery, and being the self-sufficient badass that you are, I know you're brave enough to ask for it now and then. Asking for help is also something that humbles and equalises us as human beings. It means no one is above anyone else and we can all be there to support one another as needed.

When we are asked for help by someone else, it often strengthens the bond we have with those people and I have no doubt that some of your kindest gestures will be sitting in someone's heart somewhere, right now, and that someone is just waiting for the moment to help you out, too.

I'm dreading this, but I'm ready to ask for help!

1 **Think of the countless times you have helped others**. Did you judge them? Did you think of them as weak? Or did you feel privileged and honoured to be asked to help them out. Did it even give you a little boost of confidence? Every time you want to shy away from asking for help, remind yourself of how you have felt when you've been asked.

2 **Drop the stigma you've attached to reaching out**. Every time the 'tough it out' voice rears its head, you can affirm 'Asking for help is brave and is my gift to others.'

3 **Challenge yourself to ask for help**. Start with things that have low stakes, such as asking the neighbour for a cup of washing powder or someone at work to pass on a message for you, then work your way up.

4 **Create a support bubble**. Actually have a conversation with those around you during which you all decide to actively support one another. Focus on specific areas. Perhaps you create a school run support bubble, whereby if someone is late to school one day, you can pop it in your group chat and someone will swoop in and take the pressure off. Maybe it's a work support bubble, so that if someone is finding a particular work issue a challenge, you talk it out as a group and find solutions together. You're not alone, you never were, and by showing up in this brave new way, you remind others they're not alone either.

'Asking for help is an act of bravery.'

#29

Change your
BS story

Our lives are just a series of stories, experiences and memories, sprinkled with our interpretation of them all. Things happen to us, we create some beliefs around the things that happen, and then we base our decisions going forward on what version of the story we grabbed on to.

Yet the story you came up with isn't fact, it's an opinion. There may be facts within it, but how you interpret the situation is based on your own perception of the world and what you already believed about the world at that time.

There are always many ways to look at the same moment. We all have times when we are feeling a little delicate and emotional and then someone will make a joke and it lands in the worst way. Suddenly we are crying and maybe even arguing with that person. The same joke could be said on our 'best day' and we would laugh and throw out a cheeky little comeback without incident. The situation is the same both times but how our mind filters it is different, and that is also the case with every story we tell ourselves.

The issue comes when our stories are unhelpful, and then these old negative stories taint our new, fresh moments and keep us locked in an unhappy cycle.

Imagine your life is like a book with lots of different chapters. Each chapter has its own version of you and characters you interact with.

Some characters will come with you, some will leave after chapter two and maybe even reappear again in chapter 20.

Sometimes, however, we find ourselves stuck in a chapter, re-reading it and reliving it over and over again. It's dull, it's frustrating and in order for us to have a life we love and stories to tell when we are old and grey, we must constantly be editing and making sure these stories are still serving us.

Think about your life for a moment now. How do you describe it? How do you talk about yourself and your current situation? Do you refer back to past negative stories a lot? Do you make excuses for current behaviour with reruns of the old stories as reasons for things?

Maybe it's time to make new stories.

Now I know that we don't all start off in the same place. Of course not. Some of you reading this were dealt the worst childhoods. Some of you have had experiences in your early life that would make those with lovely childhoods curl their toes.

Is there anything we can do about that imbalance in our stories? Erm, nope! So are we going to focus on that? Erm, nope.

We can acknowledge that some of us have to work a bit harder to let some old stories go (and may even require some professional therapy to help with this). But we aren't going to be resentful of those who didn't have the same negative experiences as us because everyone has their battles, and our resentment that it's 'easier for some' is helping to keep us stuck in our BS story.

After one of my speaking events, a lady came to chat to me about something she was trying to work through as she wanted some advice. This beautiful soul told me she was shy and never spoke up or felt very confident. She had deduced that this stemmed from the death of her mum at a young age and some unaddressed grief. At 28, she felt held back and stagnated by the current version of herself.

As she explained all the reasons why she was as she was, I listened intently. I asked her what she did for a job and she said that she was a secondary school teacher. She worked at a school for children who had come from challenging backgrounds and needed extra support. I encouraged her to tell me about a typical day and listened as she described having to stand in front of a class of teenagers who heckled and jeered, who didn't want to be there and who would often have quite extreme emotional outbursts.

My own version of the world felt that this was a very difficult job and required an enormous amount of patience and strength. I asked her if it took confidence to do what she did and she agreed 'absolutely' and that in her first month she didn't think she would get through it.

As we stood chatting, I encountered a strong, confident and articulate woman who was nothing like the shy and 'stuck' version of herself she'd described. I shared my observations with her and asked her which version of herself she wanted to be. At the age of 15, when her mum died, it had made sense to retreat into herself, but at 28 that version of herself was outdated.

I asked if she felt the old story was serving her and if perhaps she could find ways to let go of 'shy girl' and allow the confident teacher to emerge more forcefully. As I watched her give herself permission it was honestly like a light bulb had gone off in her head. She has since messaged me to thank me for my gentle nudge.

I share this lady's story because I think we all hold on to past versions of ourselves and forget that we are the authors of our stories, and at any point we can change what happens.

I'm ready to change my BS story, what can I do next?

1 **Work out what the story is.** Look at the tricky areas of your life and see what story you are telling yourself about them.

Who are you in this story? A victim, an aggressor, a hero? Notice the way you describe your current self and situation, and words that come up frequently.

2 **Decide what you would love the new story for your life to be** and write it down. Perhaps you had a toxic relationship and what you want is safety, love and support. Write that version out, with you as the strong hero who has solid boundaries and loves herself.

3 **Write down the current beliefs that are keeping you stuck in this story**. For example, 'If I speak up at work, I'll embarrass myself' – and then write next to it a new belief that would help you to move towards the new story you'd like to have. 'When I speak up at work it shows confidence' or 'Other people are too worried about what they have to say next to think about whether or not I will mess up.'

4 **Imagine the hero of your new story in your mind's eye** and how that person would behave. See yourself stepping into that new story and that version of yourself. As you imagine walking around in the more positive story, I want you to thank the old story for having been there when you needed it (we create all our stories to protect ourselves, we just sometimes forget they don't have to stay). Smile to yourself as you give yourself permission to move on.

'The story of your life you come up with isn't fact, it's merely an opinion.'

#30

Do nothing

When you take a snow globe and shake it up it's chaotic and wild for a moment, but if you leave it alone the snow will settle and it will be calm once more. As human beings, we sometimes need to remember that 'nothing' – leaving things alone – is also important for us.

As a solution-type person, when things get tough, I am ready for action and looking for ways to get to work, facing the challenge head-on. Being in the world of self-development and mindset work, I have an abundance of tools at my disposal and I'm ready to whip them out on any given occasion. For many situations, this is a perfect strategy and will help me navigate my current dilemma, but there are times when no words, no tools and no distractions will work and doing nothing is the way to move forwards.

Culturally, we are taught to be forward-thinking action-takers. We are praised for 'doing' over allowing events to unfold in their own space and time. Doing nothing, then, leaves us feeling ashamed or lazy, so we remain 'switched on' and constantly striving, wanting and needing.

When was the last time you did nothing? Actually nothing, though. We say we are 'doing nothing' while also binge-watching *Grey's Anatomy*, idly scrolling through social media and painting our nails. I'm talking about *nothing* nothing.

You see, nothing is a decision. You can consciously choose to 'nothing' for the day, nothing about a situation, nothing to 'fix' things. Nothing can often be the secret solution we all need.

There is a Dutch concept that I have recently been made aware of called *niksen*, which when translated means 'to be idle, do nothing or do something that has no purpose'. After reading more about this idea, I have quickly fallen in love with such a simple shift. The Western world thrives on filling our time with the notion that accomplishment, execution and activity is king, while being still is something to be scorned and scoffed at.

What if doing nothing is 100 per cent the thing required to help you feel happier. What if the feeling of always being in 'drive' mode is what's making you feel unhappy. What happens if when a situation raises its head, you didn't go into attack, doing or go mode, but instead you parked up, rode it out and did absolutely nothing for a moment before considering your next steps.

I guess there's a level of trust in doing nothing; it's not a familiar ideal for us and so it can make us feel less proactive and as if we aren't taking charge. So how about we reframe this and we take a conscious, even scheduled, moment of doing nothing with the knowledge that even in this time 'off' our brain is still working on things (in fact, studies have shown that even when in 'nothing' mode or 'daydreaming', our brain activity is as busy on MRI scans as it is when we are active).

I'll be honest and admit that the thought of doing nothing feels completely alien to me. Learning to *niks* my way through life is a fresh thought process. It's also pretty liberating. Rather than being in fight-or-flight mode when a problem arises, how about we just STOP, consider and allow time to move forwards. Rather than pushing or forcing our brain to solve things immediately, we should take our moments of nothing and trust that this action will help new solutions arise.

Some people describe *niksen* as 'permitted daydreaming' – a time to let your mind wander, ponder and contemplate the world around you. Think long walks and mindless staring out the window, with no end goal and no agenda. When we do nothing, we activate something called the default mode network (DMN) regions in our brains. It is important for us to tap into this as it is a space where our brain can reflect, consider and help us make sense of the world.

There are also studies that show that this time out for ourselves can encourage creativity and stop burnout. On a personal note, I experience it as a time to breathe and feel lighter about life. For those busy-minded folks out there (you're my people) it might take practice but even a regular time-out can greatly improve our mental health.

In modern living, our attention is diverted left, right and centre and we sometimes find our heads spinning with all of the attention-grabbing moments. The clickbait titles on YouTube that send us to videos about celebrity gossip, the eye-grabbing headlines that saw me clicking on an article from the previous day that was about a 'rubber chicken' handbag that 'everyone is obsessing over'. There are adverts on buses and billboards, sales and money-off pop-ups that turn our heads and make us think we 'need' something. Distraction is everywhere.

Now I appreciate that there will be some of you reading this and thinking, 'I don't have time to do *niksen*, so *niks* off!' But the point is exactly that. We are always trying to forcibly fix things and push through everything. You may have come to this book because you felt the need to fix yourself or find solutions and so 'doing nothing' is one I shall offer.

Let go of the control, experiment with scheduled nothing time and also take a moment to do nothing first when a problem arises, before you respond. Explore what comes up for you when 'nothing' is an option.

I'm ready to niks my day, how is it done?

1 Silence the inner voice that will tell you to 'do something useful with your time' and replace it with a nurturing voice that reminds you that your permitted daydreaming is an important part of self-care.

2 **Consciously do nothing**. Unlike mindfulness (see 'Mindful AF' on p. 136), this is not about bringing your mind back to the present, but about letting your mind wander and flow where it wants to go. The nice thing about this is that you can do it anywhere. In your car before the school run, on your lunch break or possibly during a tremendously boring meeting (just don't tell your boss I said this!).

3 **Watch**. Watch people, watch birds, watch the waves of the sea or the clouds in the sky. Find some *niks* hobbies that require no input from you.

4 **Schedule in the nothing**. If it alleviates the guilt, put it in your diary. 'I have 10 minutes to spare before the next meeting, I will do nothing.' Make sure you have 'nothing' time once every day and begin to notice the impact of this.

"What if doing nothing is 100 per cent the thing required to help you feel happier."

#31

Mindful AF

Do you ever feel that some words come out of nowhere and suddenly you see them dropped into conversation on TV chat shows and in news articles, and you're just expected to know what they mean? 'Mindfulness' feels like one of those words. I mean, don't get me wrong, as you're reading this book there's a good chance you've come across the concept of mindfulness before, but I always find it interesting how suddenly something takes hold and becomes *the* buzz word of the moment.

Yet when things become a bit more mainstream (which in this case is excellent progress), their true meaning can often get watered down, confused and lost. A friend of mine recently told me about the 'mindfulness room' that had been created at his workplace. That sounds like a very forward-thinking employer, you may be thinking, but the problem was that nobody knew what the hell mindfulness was and so it was just, well, a room (and an empty one at that!).

Mindfulness can be originally traced back to the East and has roots in Hinduism and Buddhism. In more recent years, it has made its way across to the West and more secular folks have taken its lessons and extracted the religion. When I discuss mindfulness in this chapter I mean the more Western definition, but you can add your own religious take on it too (in the same way you can to all aspects of your life).

To put it simply, mindfulness is the practice of being in the present moment, of being mindful of your surroundings, feelings and the current time. When it's stripped back like that and put in such simple terms you would be forgiven for thinking, 'Well we do that without any help, don't we?' And the answer would be, sadly, 'No'.

We spend an inordinate amount of our time living in either the past or the future. Looking longingly back to times we miss or moments we regret, or speeding towards a future self. It is pretty rare that we really stay present in the now.

When I was 20, I went to drama school (I was trying to be taken seriously as an actor, dahling), where I did a mindfulness lesson during which the teacher gave me the book *The Power of Now: A Guide to Spiritual Enlightenment* by Eckhart Tolle (Namaste Publishing, 1997). This is about how living in the present moment is the path to happiness and enlightenment, whereas living in the past or future gets in the way of genuine happiness.

Twenty-year-old me flicked through this book with the dismissiveness of youth and continued to live heavily in my future self. I was so desperate to get to the next stage of my life that the idea of being in that present moment was abhorrent to me. Having re-read Tolle's book many times since then, I understand it more deeply now.

I like to think about mindfulness as the practice of checking in with myself, of noticing how I feel in my mind and my body. When we don't check in and we avoid either physical or emotional pain or unrest, it is likely that this pain or unrest will make itself known to us in unpredictable ways.

Here's an example. Let's say that for weeks you ignore your frustration with 'annoying Anne' at work, who steals your ideas and wears too much perfume, and you swallow down your fury. This works for a while, but eventually you will be forced to acknowledge it, when you get stomach pains or you come home and scream at your husband.

When we don't check in with our physical bodies, the same rules apply. If we sit hunched over our laptops all day without addressing our posture, it's likely that one day we'll wake up with a bad back and tension headaches.

If we adopt a more mindful attitude to living, however, we can catch this stuff way before it gets to the point of us losing our heads or needing to seek out a doctor.

Mindfulness is not complicated. This is one of the reasons I love it as a tool. We can all practise mindfulness wherever and whenever we wish, without the need for a 'mindful room' or spiritual guidance. Indeed, it is a scientifically proven way to reduce stress, anxiety and let go of the daily tensions of life.

I want to be present, what do I do?

1 **Mindful moments**. Factor a mindful moment into each day. If you've never done this before, choose a time, set an alarm on your phone and get to work. Perhaps it's while you have your morning coffee or during your lunch break. Whenever you do it, here are the steps to follow:

1. Do a mental body scan, from head to toe, asking yourself to relax each part of your body. Pay particular attention to problem areas, such as a tense forehead, jaw, shoulders and hands.

2. Once you've done the body scan, become aware of your surroundings and the moment you are in.

   What can you smell? What can you taste? What can you hear? What can you feel? What can you see?

3. Notice your breath going in and out, not trying to manipulate it or change it, just being aware of it.

4. Finally, ask yourself, 'How am I today?' And notice what comes up for you.

2 **Mindfully eat**. For those who have often found themselves in battles with their food, practising mindfully eating is a great habit to bring into your life. As you take a bite, become aware of smells, tastes, textures and each chew of the food.

3 **Mindfully shower**. Use this time in the morning to notice the sensation of the water across your body. Is it hot or cold? What can you hear as your shower (for me it's often the gentle sound of my daughters screaming at each other and fighting over who has the last of a cereal).

4 **Walk mindfully**. How often have you raced to your destination without thought? On my school run with my daughters we will play 'Let's spot something we have never seen before'. We walk to school the same way every day but, interestingly, we always find something new.

5 **Understand that practising mindfulness does not mean that you are devoid of thoughts or emotions**. It does not mean that your 'inner critic voice' will not show up. What it does mean, though, is that when the voice in your head is unhelpful, you will notice it more quickly and be able to deal with it at source (check out 'You're being a bully to yourself' on p. 44, in which I discuss the inner critic).

'The moment that you are in right now is the only thing that is real. Be in it fully.'

#32

Stop being so damn 'judgy'

My name is Holly Matthews and I am a former very 'judgy' person (who's doing her best to change!). Zip back to just a few years ago and I now see that I was extremely judgemental. Saying that out loud feels a bit shameful; it's not a trait any of us want to admit to, but I'll hazard a guess that I may not be the only one.

And yet I certainly didn't think of myself as being judgemental. I saw myself as a person with strong opinions who wasn't afraid to show up and be heard. I had *my* model of the world, the way I saw things, and when I saw others living outside of these parameters, I judged.

I'll be honest here and say that even as an open person, who likes to speak her truth, my toes are curling as I write this down. It's embarrassing to admit when you didn't get something right, but equally I can't write this book and not share my own personal journey of discovery.

My judgement centred around not wanting people to do things in a more 'traditional' way. Go to school, maybe university, get a nine-to-five job, live for the weekend, get married and settle down. I had grown up trying to push against what the social norms were, the things we are 'supposed' to do, and although I was trying to teach people they could live their life *their* way, I was actually projecting that they could live their life *my* way. It was always done with the best of intentions – wanting people to understand that there are other options, and I stand by that ethos – but very often I was sitting firmly up on my high horse telling people that their way was wrong.

What stopped this judgement loop was my husband becoming sick and then dying. This rocked the foundations of what I knew to be true about the world, and I met and received messages from so many people going through similar things (from all walks of life, both employed and 'traditional' in their lives and also the against-the-grain types). It made me recognise there are many ways to exist and we all go through stuff in our own way, just trying to find our path. It released my judgement of the differences.

I know some of you will be thinking, 'but everyone judges, it's part of life' and you'd be right, judgement is a fundamental feature of human beings. However, be wary of finding yourself in a perpetual cycle of pessimistic judgement of *everything*, because that's hard to get out of and you are training your brain to look for the worst. While in judgement mode, we make snap decisions and condemn the world, while also internally judging and condemning ourselves for all the judging we are doing.

If you judge the flustered single mum on the school run (it's me, I'm the flustered single mum on the school run!), you likely also judge your neighbour, the celeb of the moment, the person from school who posts cryptic messages on Facebook, your friends, your family and, without a doubt, yourself. Often, how we do one thing is how we do everything, and judgement of others leads to judgement of yourself and the assumption that everyone else is judging you just as harshly.

Let's look at why you're doing the judging. What does judgement give you? Every action we take has a motivation and it might be worth looking at whether this judgement has become pure habit or if there's another underlying reason.

Do you judge as a way to bond with a group, for example? Do you judge others because it gives you a feeling of superiority? Take a moment to look inwards and see what you can discover. Commonly, we judge in others what we dislike about ourselves, and while you're pointing and wagging your finger at others, your ego feels elevated and you're distracted from dealing with any underlying feelings of not being good enough.

Wouldn't it feel nicer to let go of the weight of having to judge others so harshly? What about if the next time you felt the desire to, you questioned the motivation to do it and considered whether you could say something positive instead (see also 'Watch your mouth' on p. 120).

Nobody sets out to be the judgemental one and I hope that as you read this and perhaps notice some of your own actions in this chapter you'll be ready for some ideas on how to change...

The judgement 'shake off'

1 **Challenge the thoughts**. If you hear yourself saying, 'She has awful hair' or 'Why doesn't that mum stop her children running around the restaurant?', stop and notice the judgement and focus your attention immediately on something good about the person or consider what else might be going on: 'She has a nice smile' or 'She might be having a really tough time, I wonder if I could offer to help.'

2 **Walk in their shoes for a moment**. Last year, my daughters and I parked across the road from a lady's house. I parked legally, I was in the right, but this lady tapped on my window and asked me to leave. She was rude and unreasonable and my initial reaction was to have a disagreement with her and defend my corner. Through my lens of snap judgement, this woman had spoiled my morning, had made my girls cry and was an awful human. What I learned later from a neighbour was that this woman's husband was very ill and quite recently someone had blocked her drive and an ambulance had been unable to get through. It appears that this woman was worried that might happen again, and with everything going on in her world, she had misdirected her fury, so I bore the brunt of someone else's

mistake. Having my own experience of what it's like to look after a sick husband, I was able to walk in her shoes and understand her point of view, defusing my judgement and anger. At the time I knew I hadn't done anything wrong, and I didn't have the full story, so I stood up for myself accordingly. On later finding out the full situation it was a stark reminder that we have no idea what fires other people are fighting and I was able to tap into pure compassion for her outburst.

3 Acknowledge your own ugly corners and dark shadows.
Appreciate that you don't always get stuff right and that we are all messy, imperfect and doing our best. By being honest about your own failings or weaknesses it's easier to understand that others have them too and to be kinder in your approach.

4 Remind yourself what it feels like to be on the receiving end of such judgement
before dishing it out like judgement candy. We all have that one person we know who wants to moralise about some topic or other, their accusing tone spewing damnation at you, and we don't like it! It's OK for others to live their lives differently, for you to not like what they do, and to have all the opinions you wish, but if you spend too much time in the judgement vortex you're going to be sucked into it and feel rubbish.

5 Get curious.
Consider why you are feeling the urge to judge. What are you feeling inside? Is there envy or jealousy, are you angry about something, do you feel anxious? Perhaps you don't feel good enough and on closer inspection the judgement makes you feel 'better than'?

'It's OK for others to live their lives differently.'

#33

Be more boring

Life goals are sexy.

They're loud, flashy and bring with them the promise of rewards and celebrations. Read a copy of any magazine at the beginning of January and it will be packed with goal-setting advice and tips on finding the motivation to get you started.

Setting audacious goals is wonderful – I have even written a chapter on them (*see* 'Set big fat goals' on p. 40). However, without what we will be discussing in *this* chapter (spoiler alert: it's habits) you will take way longer to achieve these bigger goals (if you ever do).

Habits are not sexy.

Habits are dull. But it's their humdrum regularity that will take an idea that you write on your New Year's resolution list and make it a reality.

If I look back on my life I can see that I've spent most of my time trying to crayon outside the lines. A non-conventional job, the excitement of not knowing what I'll be doing next, and always leaning into my weird. This can be fun and, with a bit of youthful bravado chucked into the mix, it can mean that you *do* smash through some of those powerful goals.

However, as I've grown up I've realised that spontaneity gets me to a point but only so far. Alongside all the good I may have achieved with this approach I have experienced a ton of chaos and disorder too, which often leaves me having to try again to finally get to where I want to be. This is where habits can help.

Habits are the tiny things we do every day that impact the bigger picture of our lives. This could be a positive thing or it could be the reason you've gained 10lb in the last couple of months and still haven't finished an assignment.

In the past, I would have resisted a schedule, sameness or systems because it would have felt tedious, but I was wrong. If we can get the foundations right, the stuff we do on autopilot, then we actually free up space to be spontaneous and wild without messing up the bigger picture and taking us away from the goals we want to achieve.

It's taken me a long time to understand the compound effect of the stuff we already do without thinking, but having recently become obsessed with habit creation and having seen the results of this, I am now on board.

For example, I'm messy. I have spent years creating chaos in my wake and then getting so annoyed by my own mess that I give my house a big spring clean once a month, promising myself I will be 'better once it's done'. I am not 'better once it's done'. I continue with the same bad habits, and the next month, half my wardrobe is once more strewn all over the floor.

Knowing this about myself, I began experimenting with micro habits, which over the last year have totally transformed my way of living. Making myself do a quick tidy before bedtime and implementing a better system of when I clean or where things go has meant that I have started to feel lighter and more in control.

So, how do we create habits?

Habits are formed in a part of our brain called the basal ganglia and our decision-making is made in our prefrontal cortex (at the front of the brain). When we first start learning to do something we have to very consciously do that thing, but over time and with repetition, this behaviour becomes habitual and the decision-making part of our brain can take a little nap (while the basal ganglia takes charge in the background).

Imagine learning to drive. When you first start driving you think about every movement of the gears, the pedals and the indicator, and it's exhausting. When I passed my test (second attempt), I was very pregnant and needed to be in Essex the next day to perform the role of Jasmin in an *Aladdin* pantomime. This journey involved driving 160km (100 miles) from my home in Coventry via the M1 and M25. For those who are unaware of these motorways, they're very busy and very fast. To say I was 'aware' of my driving is an understatement and when I saw the sign for Essex I audibly shouted, 'Yes!' as the cold sweat poured off my body...

I've since driven on those motorways hundreds of times. The act of driving regularly has become a habit, so I now no longer think about the basics of driving so intently, which frees up my mind to sing along to Alicia Keys with my kids in the back and to navigate heavy traffic with relative ease.

Whether they are good or bad habits, we form them in the same way. We get a cue to do something (for example, walking into the break room at work and smelling coffee), which triggers a routine or action (we make a coffee) and finally we receive a reward (we drink a coffee, the caffeine hits and we step the day up a notch!).

This works the same for every habitual behaviour. So, the way to shift the habits we don't want is to aim to recognise the reward we get for the behaviour and find a healthier or more beneficial reward for the same cue.

Let's say the cue to text your ex-boyfriend is coming home from a drunken night out, and the reward for the routine of the text (which you will regret in the morning) is that you get attention, you feel wanted and it's exciting. Perhaps the key to moving away from this cycle is to find another way to get that emotional support and attention – by making the new routine that you text your best friend or your sister until the cue or craving to do the routine dissipates.

The most important thing about habit creation is that it's all about the tiny changes we make every day. The reality, though, is that it will often be a long time before we see the results of the new habits, and this is when we need to decide who we want to be.

If I decide that I want to be a healthy woman who exercises regularly and stops eating so many biscuits, then I need to look at the habits I have already and where they can be tweaked. I must come back to who it is I want to be and remember this every time I feel like slumping back into my old behaviours.

If you'd like more of a deep dive into this topic then I recommend you check out James Clear's *Atomic Habits: Tiny Changes, Remarkable Results* (Penguin Random House, 2018), which looks specifically at habit creation. Or if you're ready to get started with changes *now*, you'll find my quick and easy starting prompts below.

OK, I want good habits, where do I start?

1 **Decide how you'd like your life to look and who you want to be**. Perhaps you want to be a person who reads regularly, who's more social or maybe you are seeking a better work–life balance? Don't censor your choices, just decide. Then write a list of the habits that will take you closer to your goals and the habits that are currently keeping you from them. Use 'habit stacking' ideas, i.e. 'When I do this, I also do that.' For example, 'When I boil the kettle, I do 10 sit-ups.'

2 **Write down alternative rewards** for the current bad habits, and make them easy and obvious. A client of mine wasn't getting a good balance of her food intake: every time she came home, she would eat slices of ham out of the fridge (sometimes a whole packet in one sitting). It had become so habitual that the moment she dropped her bag on the table she looked for her reward. Once she recognised this, she prepped some healthier options and moved the ham out of reach. The fact that she could still eat *something* was enough to help her start changing the habit.

3 **Take away choices from your day**. Create a 'uniform' or dress code, a meal plan that you repeat, and stick to the same times to do things each day. The more we do things on repeat, the less our brain has to think (which is what exhausts and overwhelms us). Mark Zuckerberg famously wears the same T-shirt every day and explains it's because he wants to make as few decisions as possible so he can best serve his community at work.

4 **Start small with new habits and keep going**. This isn't about huge leaps, it's about truly becoming the person you want to be. Keep going until you stop congratulating yourself for the behaviour. That's when you know it's truly 'who you are' now.

‹The "boring" repetition of habit creates space for spontaneity and excitement.›

#34

Be ruthless with your inner circle

I don't have many friends.

Now that might make me sound lonely, but I don't see it as a negative. Those whom I have chosen to include in my life are truly excellent people and I'm incredibly lucky to have them.

When it comes to our mental health and feeling good, being selective about whom you spend time with isn't such a bad notion. In fact, there have been many studies into whether (as the old adage states) 'we are the average of the five people we spend the most time with', a quote attributed to American entrepreneur Jim Rohn. Results do show that the influence people have on us is substantial and actually goes way further than just our closest five people, as even our friend's, friend's, friend's levels of happiness can filter down and impact us.

This means that not only do we have to check out who we spend most of our time with but also who our friends choose to spend their time with. I appreciate, realistically, this may be hard to influence but it's certainly worth understanding how important choosing friends wisely needs to be.

Those we invite into our most intimate circle have the most influence over our behaviours. A 1999 study branded this the 'Michelangelo effect'. Just as Michelangelo would sculpt his works of art, the study found that a supportive partner can help transform or 'sculpt' you into the person they see. A partner who champions you by telling you how smart you are, for example, might well give you the encouragement you need to complete the degree you keep putting on hold. The beauty your partner sees in your post-pregnancy body might begin to filter into your mind and allow you to see it too when you look in the mirror.

Of course, on the flip side of this study is a stark warning. If your inner circle, or someone in it, doesn't believe in you or has doubts about your abilities then you will likely soak up this messaging too and begin to believe it. For example, a client of mine had a partner who berated her business ideas for years, mostly due to his own fears, and this discouraged my client from following her dreams. His doubt had seeped into her. And yet when they split up, the veil of fear dissolved and she created the very business he had told her she couldn't.

Having positive influences in our world can really support us in being our best selves. It can help us be inspired and will shift how we approach everything. The cheerleading companions will help you feel motivated and there are even studies that show that a strong friendship circle can add years to your life. Being part of a group is in some way a very human need and, as I look back on my life, I see clearly both the positive and negative groups I have been part of.

At 14, my friends and I would dress alike. It was a conscious decision to feel part of a group and our particular 'tribe' wore fake Burberry skirts and often matching shirts. I know, I know, it was a strong look and we owned it. It made us feel that sense of togetherness and in turn affected how I was perceived by the outside world. Had I hung out with the 'grungy' kids (all in black with piercings) I would no doubt have begun to morph into their style, and again, the world's perception of me would have been different.

What we wear and how we connect in our tribes may be a seemingly trivial thing to note but it's a good example of how quickly we start to resort to primal behaviours of wanting to be 'in' and part of a group, and how this may impact the world's reaction to us and the decisions we make.

Not everyone wants or needs many friends and that's OK. It's all about quality over quantity in the friendship game: it's far better to have a couple of marvellous friends than a bunch of toxic ones who don't align with who you want to be.

Look at your current group and consider whether they match up with who you are at this point in your life. Or perhaps you have drifted away and no longer have much in common? It doesn't mean you never will again, just that it may not be the caring and supportive circle you currently need.

I'm ready to build my circle of inspiring cohorts, where do I start?

1 **Create a checklist of things that are important to you in a friend**. Many people do this for romantic relationships when they click on to dating sites, but forget that the same rules apply in our friendships too. This could be 'must show an interest in my life and the things I like', 'must lack judgement', 'must accept me as I am' or 'must love *Sex and the City* as much as I do'. Your choice, your checklist.

2 **Audit your current circle**. I'm not saying we never see them again, but at this moment in your life it's worth tuning in and seeing who you would like to spend more or less time with. Ask yourself: 'Am I able to be my best self around this person?', 'Do I leave this person's presence and feel uplifted or deflated, supported or chastised?', 'Do I trust this person and both respect and get respect from them?'

3 **Nurture the important friendships**. I am going to read this sentence to myself and let it sit with me too, because it's so easy to just let each day tick by and find you've not contacted those you care deeply about for weeks. Send a text, post a letter, organise a meet-up and reignite the joy in your friendship.

'Your tribe impacts your vibe.
Choose wisely!'

#35

Big girls DO cry

I'm a crier.

I cry at commercials and movies. I sob uncontrollably at *Grey's Anatomy* and I cry when I'm sad. I am always the weepy one with tissues at a wedding. I cry when I listen to incredible singers (there's a scene in *Sister Act 2* in which Lauryn Hill sings by the piano and even writing about this is choking me up), and I cry when I'm happy.

I am a big advocate of crying, a super fan even.

Unfortunately, though, there are so many negative connotations linked to crying that many people do not share my view. For instance, we may have been taught as a child to 'suck it up' or that it's 'weak to cry', so for some of us, crying may bring about shame and embarrassment.

In popular mental health conversations, we hear the phrase 'it's OK not to be OK' bandied around all over the place, but it doesn't often *feel* 'OK not to be OK' when it comes to our outward displays of emotion.

I once offered up the advice to my then eight-year-old daughter that if she felt sad at school she should take some time to go to the toilet and have a little cry. Her answer was categorically 'No chance, absolutely not!' Because even at that young age she had learned that this would be deemed 'embarrassing'.

Do you relate to this? Do you feel uncomfortable with the idea of crying? If so, then by the end of the chapter my aim is to show you that crying is actually beneficial for your mental health and can be used as a tool to help you feel good.

So, let's begin with the basics. What are tears anyway?

Essentially there are three types:

1. **Basal**: The general wetness of our eyes that keeps them moist. It's protein-rich and antibacterial (I now feel like a QVC presenter, trying to sell you tears).

2. **Reflex**: You've chopped an onion – stuff's about to get wild in your eyes! That's your body's reaction to clearing out anything that may irritate them.

3. **Emotional**: Life happens, the tears flow. These tears contain stress hormones, which means that when we cry we are literally crying out the stress.

Learning this about the 'emotional' tears blows my mind. Why aren't we taught this? Our tears are helping us clear away our stress, so keeping them in means the stress stays in. Honestly, having this on the school syllabus would definitely have helped me more than learning how to make rock buns in food technology.

In Japan, they recognise the need to help people to relieve their stresses and let out their tears. Culturally, outward displays of emotion are frowned upon, and so in recent years 'crying clubs' have sprung up as a way to help people to cry. These clubs are called *rui-katsu*, which translates as 'tear-seeking'. Groups will gather together and are encouraged to grant themselves permission to feel the trickle of hot tears on their faces. It is seen as a pragmatic way of dealing with their mental health.

Crying is also important as it helps to signal to those around us that something is wrong, and it helps us to elicit support and seek out care. Your colleague at work might look 'fine' but when you see her sobbing at her desk, it's a clear signal for you to check in and see what's wrong.

I know that some of you are probably thinking, 'I'm never going to cry at my desk Holly, get a grip' and that's because how we feel about crying is on a spectrum. Some people sit on the 'I will never cry, I am a fortress' side, while others cry every time they need help. As with most things, balance is key. If the crying feels out of control, endless and leaves us needing other people to pick up the pieces every time then we won't feel very empowered by our tears. Equally, if we never cry and we swallow down our emotions then we'll find that this also disempowers us in a different way.

What is your crying 'story'? Did you see your parents cry? Do you feel comfortable crying? Were tears 'safe' in your home? What do you feel when you see others cry?

I was lucky in that I saw both my parents cry and be vulnerable in a healthy way. I never thought it weird that my dad sobbed at *It's a Wonderful Life* every Christmas and I was never made to feel small for my big emotions. Plus, as an actress, I had to cry on demand and that actually gave me an understanding of what triggers those emotions within me.

Not all of you will see crying as a tool for positivity yet, but hopefully after this chapter you will understand the benefits. Crying is our body's way of helping ourselves, so if we stifle this natural coping mechanism because of some crazy societal pressure to appear 'strong' and have our lives in order, then we are walking ourselves into a ton of pain and wasting a natural resource that can help us feel good. Together, let's make a stand to embrace the tears.

Fetch me the tissues, I'm ready to cry

1 **Understand your story**. Answer the questions I asked in this chapter and get to know your own personal 'crying story'. The more we have clues about how we got to this point, the quicker we can get to where we want to be.

2 **Speak kindly to yourself when you cry**. Rather than 'You're too sensitive', 'It's not even a big deal, why are you crying?' or 'You're so pathetic', try 'Crying is brave', 'I am strong enough to be vulnerable' and 'Crying is my self-care' to empower yourself. If we chastise ourselves during our sobbing then this can stop us from benefiting. Listen carefully next time the flood gates open.

3 **Engineer the tears**. If you're struggling to release your own emotions then watching a sad film, listening to music or reading about someone else's sadness can help you to cry vicariously, and that's still beneficial.

4 **Remember you *can* 'cry over spilt milk'**. You are allowed to cry for reasons that seem 'small'. The moment you cry, guilt-free, because life got a bit tough (however big or small the problem) is the moment the tears help you feel refreshed and able to try again.

'Tears contain stress hormones, which means that when we cry we are literally crying away our stress.'

#36

Celebrate your victories

As I've mentioned, when I was 19 I signed a record contract with a record label. I was in their London offices and my manager, Matt, was cheering by my side. I signed the contract and was handed a glass of champagne.

I don't remember too much about the day but I do remember exactly how I felt: empty. I was without any of 'my people' and all I could think was 'I haven't done anything to warrant celebrating yet.'

I'd achieved something yet I felt flat. Does that sound familiar?

On one hand, I was kinda right, because I hadn't released any music yet and I was very early on in any journey to 'musical superstardom'. But on the other hand, I was missing some glaringly obvious considerations.

To sign a record deal *is* a big deal. And it was with one of the leading record companies in the world. Just to get a meeting with them is a huge achievement.

I'd met with numerous other record companies and had had many meetings to get to this moment. I had also been a performer for more than 10 years and had honed my craft through hundreds of lessons and during hours of work on TV sets. So, in reality, I'd put in the time and I did deserve to pat myself on the back to mark this moment.

Of course I appreciate this example is extreme and not what the average everyday win looks like (it's not even *my* everyday win), but I'm using this example to show that even if and when we do hit these extremes, the challenges we face in appreciating our achievements are just the same.

As my journey unfolded I never did hit the dizzy heights of musical greatness and so my mindset at that time spoiled an important moment for me. Over the years, this story has been repeated for every win in my life. When I bought my first house or got my first client, for example, I didn't take those moments in. Why not? For the same reasons we all struggle:

- The current win is unlikely to be the end goal – the big fat bigger-picture goal. You feel that celebrating the tiny win is a waste of time until you've hit the huge goal.
- You may feel that celebrating or shouting about your success is egotistical and tacky. Perhaps you were brought up to be modest and not shout about your achievements.
- Maybe you don't feel like there is time to celebrate because you've already hurled yourself on to the next thing, having barely had time to catch your breath, let alone clap for this fleeting triumph.

Whatever the reason for avoiding a little 'well done me', I want to help you to see why this has to change.

One of the first things to consider as I steer you towards celebrating is that the big goals we have in life rarely happen overnight. In order to keep going when it gets hard, it's helpful to notice each milestone and develop an addiction to the progress. Imagine a fitness goal. You're training for that marathon – something that takes preparation and practice and doesn't happen overnight. Our big goals, whatever they are, will have the same trajectory. We might have to do some actual training to get to our dream career, or practise a particular skill, then take it stage by stage, congratulating ourselves at each milestone, glancing back to see how far we've already come to spur us on to the finish line.

You see, the journey to the goal is itself also the win. We can never fully appreciate the massive accomplishments if we haven't also experienced hardships along the way. We need to remind ourselves that the process matters to the full picture.

Acknowledging your wins also naturally brings you into the present moment, which if you've read 'Mindful AF' on p. 136 you'll be aware is beneficial to our happiness. Noticing your tiny daily breakthroughs as you go can bring moments of joy and appreciation that hugely impact your mood.

Now, of course, I am not saying all of our celebrations must be in public (in fact most will be merely in your head) but by openly sharing your jubilation you can also inspire others to find theirs. Just this week, a woman in The Happy Me Project membership group shared her pride in having quit smoking and five others instantly created a group to support each other to do the same. No matter who you are, you have no idea how important your words and your wins can be in motivating others to find theirs.

When we talk about and share our wins, our 'happy' hormones oxytocin, serotonin and dopamine show up in abundance too, which makes us feel good *and* motivated to seek out more of the same.

It's important to remember at this point that I am not only talking about 'wins' in the context of the 'big wins' but also the 'everyday wins'. It really depends where you are in your world at this present moment.

If recently life has felt heavy and a bit crap, then a win for you might be eating a meal and getting dressed. If you've mastered the art of clean hair and putting on pants then perhaps it's handing in that bit of work, tidying the garden or even asking someone out on a date. Wins are wins and we need to stop minimising them because we are comparing them with someone else's. (*See also* 'Comparison' on p. 186.)

It's fairly obvious we should celebrate the massive wins, but hey, I know some of you just did something most would consider a huge achievement and you brushed over it like it was small. I know this because I have done this as well. This is an ongoing process for me too and I still work hard on cheerleading myself on.

No more minimising how challenging being an adult is. It stops today. From now on, we are going to clap loudly for ourselves for whatever reason we want. We are in the arena of training our brains to focus on the good so that our brains begin to seek out more of the same, and celebration is an important tool for doing this.

Fetch the party poppers, I'm ready to cheer for myself!

1 **The 'win' book**. Get yourself a notebook and each night before you sleep I want you to write down three things you did that day that meant you were winning.

2 **Talk about your wins with those around you**. Make it a habit among your friends to share your 'weekly wins'. Basking in your friends' wins and getting their positive feedback about your own will feel lovely. It will also help focus your attention on your achievements and in turn will lead to more of the same.

3 **Reward even the small milestones**. Create a rewards list of things you love to do and when you tick off another win, choose a prize. We see this as the pastime of children, but we love trophies, stickers and lollies as much as kids (although stickers may change to 'going to the cinema' and lollies might be 'cocktails with friends').

"Clap for every small win, to get to the big win quicker."

#37

Feeling like a fraud

In around 2004, I was standing on an empty stage, staring out at a crowd of a few thousand people. Lights, cameras and expectation. I was booked to do one of my first performances as a solo singer, at a huge charity event. At this point, I had no identity as a singer and was very awkward around the whole thing.

A week before, I had been at Pineapple Dance Studios in London rehearsing with a top choreographer and performance coach. Even though I'd been an actress for many years, I had always found singing to be a very vulnerable and personal experience. My journey to becoming a singer was not something I had chased, and had only come about after my character on a TV show had begun singing and I was scouted. Real life imitating art.

During the rehearsal I was incredibly nervous and kept taking breaks to let off steam (and sometimes to cry). I was so uncomfortable and doubting of myself that I could have been physically sick. I've only recently shared this story with my friends and family and they confessed they'd never have guessed that's how I was feeling at the time.

Being in front of that crowd felt like one of those awful dreams in which you're naked on a stage with everyone you know in the audience. My face was beaming red and my heart was thumping so loudly it seemed like it could have been outside my chest. It felt like the worst performance of my life and I couldn't have felt any less deserving of being there if I had tried.

This isn't the only time I've felt like this. My career has been very fluid and there have definitely been times when I've 'thrown a lot of mud at the wall until some of it sticks'. I've done many things and because of this I developed the belief I was a 'jack of all trades, master of none'. Even as recently as two years ago, I was still carrying the belief that I was winging it and somewhat undeserving of all that I have created.

I could pick up an award for my work, be invited to prestigious events with highly esteemed people (even sit right beside them), and yet inside I just didn't see myself on the same page.

I know I'm not alone in this feeling because it comes up with nearly every client I work. There's a name for it – imposter syndrome.

You may have experienced the 'I shouldn't be here, I'm not good enough' feeling I describe above, perhaps at work, during education, or even as a mum or a partner. I'm going to bet that there have been moments of uncertainty and doubt at some point in most people's lives.

Imposter syndrome is identified as an internal experience of not believing you're as good as others perceive you to be. The feeling of being a fraud, a phoney or undeserving. You imagine that at any moment you'll be 'found out' and people will realise you simply shouldn't be where you are, or have what you have.

Like all limiting beliefs, this one will hugely impact your life and your levels of happiness, and just like every other limiting belief, even when you become aware of its existence, it will still spring up now and then when something triggers it.

Mine was triggered very recently, and boy was I surprised by how much. I had an email forwarded to me by a friend – a request from a radio journalist who wanted to speak to a 'businesswoman' who had succeeded in their work during 2020. I chat on radio shows fairly regularly and this kind of request was nothing unusual, so I breezily emailed the journalist to introduce myself.

The email I got back knocked me for six and I found myself spiralling into an imposter syndrome abyss. 'Thank you for getting in contact, but we're looking for a businesswoman.'

Instantly, I fell back into old stories running through my mind: 'See, you're not a businesswoman, you got here by luck' and 'No one is going to take you seriously' and 'You're just playing at being a businesswoman.'

Thankfully, since I now understand what this feeling is, I was able to step back from the 'clutching my pearls' moment of affront I experienced, and breathe. I looked at the facts:

1. I run a business.
2. I am a woman.
3. I have a Ltd company.
4. I get paid for my work.

Concluding then that I did fit the criteria of being a businesswoman, I recognised that these thoughts were just imposter syndrome being awoken from his slumber, provoked by a rather ill-informed journalist.

Those of us who have these feelings of being a fraud are in good company. In fact, imposter syndrome used to be seen as an 'affliction' of primarily highly successful women. Some of our imposter sisters who have shared their experience publicly are: Michelle Obama, Lady Gaga, Emma Watson, Tina Fey, Meryl Streep, Jennifer Lopez and Natalie Portman. I have ended the list here, but as you can see, it's full of people we can comfortably acknowledge have been pretty successful in their lives.

What this means is that if we don't do the inner work on this insidious imposter syndrome then it doesn't matter how many accolades we receive or how loud the applause is, it's possible that sometimes we will feel like we simply aren't good enough.

I wanna shake away my inner charlatan, what's the plan of action?

1 **Face up to the fact that imposter syndrome is showing up for you**. Acknowledge it and bring it into the light.

2 **Reframe**. Not everything about this feeling is bad. If you feel like you're not quite hitting the mark you're likely to work harder and learn more than anyone around you. You're likely to have a growth mindset (the mindset of someone who is willing to learn, develop themselves and remain optimistic) and be less 'stuck' than those who don't feel like an imposter. Perhaps imposter syndrome is your superpower. Change the dialogue.

3 **Fact vs fiction**. When the feelings show up, focus on the facts and forget the emotional landmine that may have been triggered. Facts not feelings. Write down all of the reasons you're excellent in whichever area your imposter voice gets loud. Keep this list to hand as a reminder.

4 **Take action**. Every time you show up for yourself, learn more and create a lovely life for yourself, you train your brain to understand who you really are. Eventually, the facts are too obvious for even the most well-practised imposter syndrome veteran to ignore.

> **'Every time you take action and show up for yourself, you** train your brain to understand who you really are.**'**

#38

Some days are crap

I burned some toast today. I haven't burned toast in a long time and it really annoyed me. I couldn't be bothered to wait for more toast, so I did that thing when you try to scrape off the black bits, which get everywhere, and you end up trying to fish it out of the butter (while also wishing you'd just binned the offending toast in the first place).

After burning the toast, with the sound of my children arguing about who got the last yoghurt, I stood on a piece of Lego. I know, such a cliché. Yet there I was, yelping in my kitchen in some kind of 'bad morning' satire.

Some days are crap.

Self-development isn't about being in a constant state of blissful, robotic happiness, and if that is your aim then you'll be sadly disappointed. It's helpful to recognise the highs and lows of life and to notice (and possibly even laugh at) the absurdities.

The key to getting through our 'standing on Lego days' is to remain hopeful. It's about not allowing the difficult moments or days to spiral out into crap weeks or months to come.

As I discuss in 'Don't give up' on p. 52, hope is important. The phrase 'false hope' annoys me. Hope is the thing that can drag our sorry selves through life on the days that just feel heavy. Hope isn't about delusional wishful thinking and crossing your fingers, it's about knowing how you'd like something to be and being open to the possibility that everything could work out.

You know that feeling you get when you've had a headache for a long time and then after hydrating, popping a paracetamol and praying to the 'God of headaches', it finally goes? There's a moment of bliss when you're finally pain-free, and life just feels great.

When we are in the crap moments it's important for us to remember that in the not-so-distant future we will breathe easier again. You will sigh with relief that the 'headache' of a day is over and good things are on the horizon.

Of course, a new crap day is also a dead cert at some point in the future, but we have to stop instantly reminding ourselves of this, as the opposite is also true – good days are coming.

It's important to stop fixating on these crap days to avoid the slippery slope of catastrophising every traffic jam, missed train or smashing-your-favourite-mug moment, as we can easily slip into the habit of focusing on the daily annoyances.

We can stop this pattern by taking a step back when you're having a bad day and slowing down for a moment before making the next move. If you're in your day of doom right now, take 10 full breaths and don't move another muscle. Ten, nine, eight, seven, six, five, four, three, two, one. Bring your awareness back into the room, placing your feet firmly on the ground. Now, what do you need to do next?

It's not taboo to have a bad day. If you ask any human on the planet they will unleash their 'worst day' tales upon you, helping you to recognise it's OK if some days don't hit the gold standard. It's part of life and our only job is to work out how we handle them when they arise. Luckily for you, my top tips on this are on the next page.

My day feels crap, how do I bounce back?

1 Be compassionate to yourself. Place your hand on your heart and say to yourself, 'It's OK that you're having a bad day, you're doing your best.' Being kind to ourselves in these moments is key. You are not going to berate yourself to happiness. Giving ourselves permission to be peeved is actually a big relief for many of us.

2 STOP and change the course of events. The *Sliding Doors* moments we have in our lives give us choices. In the moment you just deleted a work document you hadn't saved and the woman at the next desk is boring you with stories about her cat Tiddles, you can choose to stop and adjust the day or you can smash up your computer and scream at 'cat woman'. The choice is yours, but one way is definitely going to aid the spiral of stress. Reminding ourselves that we do have options shows there's light at the end of the tunnel and gives reassurance that solutions can be found.

3 Decompress. I'm not for one second saying you aren't going to lose your head once in a while, so knowing what will help you to decompress before you go ballistic can be a huge help. Do you need to scream obscenities into a cushion, run it off or listen to some angry hip hop in a darkened room? While researching this chapter I found a website some of you might like – https://shitday.de – where you can decompress by watching things explode (I won't judge if you love it!).

4 Get real with yourself. It's nice and comforting to lean right into the vexed feeling when something bad happens and to then add and exaggerate everything that follows. Instead of taking this easy action, say out loud exactly what's happened – 'I stood on a piece of Lego' – over and over again until it loses all meaning, and might even begin to sound a little absurd. Perspective can help us handle the daily grievances.

5 **Count the tiny joys**. When the day is of the disastrous variety, we have to savour the tiny moments of pleasure, and so I challenge you on these days to counter the crap by noticing the nice. This is an important tool all the time, but on the bad days it's non-negotiable. Keep a tally of each and every second of glee, love and harmony (perhaps even write down each one in the notes on your phone), so by the end of the day you can remind yourself that it wasn't all bad.

'It's not taboo to have a bad day and it's OK if some days don't hit the gold standard.'

#39

The art of overthinking

Albert Einstein was an overthinker.

Of course, Einstein died a long time ago and we can't ask him exactly how his brain processed everything, but based on what's written and his (on-record) obsessive nature, we can definitely conclude that the man who discovered the theory of relativity (after many failed attempts), was an overthinker. In fact, if we look at any area of 'success', we can find people who have overthought things into reality.

In daily life, though, when we talk about overthinking it is very much framed as a negative – with a focus on the overwhelm, the indecisiveness, the second guessing and the self-doubt that are all often associated with it. If you consider yourself an overthinker then you've probably already come to that conclusion, after experiencing bouts of exhaustion and having wasted hours ruminating over a situation and then probably not got stuff done as a result (because you have been too busy considering every possible outcome).

Sound familiar?

Of course there are times when we all overthink more than we would normally. This could be planning your wedding or preparing for that job interview. We want to get something right, so we plan and think about it endlessly.

This is normal and likely doesn't impact you for any significant length of time. If, however, you have slipped into the habit of overthinking *everything* you do, then it can get pretty hard to make decisions about anything (and even when you do take action, you'll then spend more time overthinking the what-ifs of the choices you've made).

Sometimes when we overthink (and I say 'we', because I'm here with you, this is my world), we convince ourselves that we are just being savvy and prepared, and that by running through things in our head we are problem solving. But there's a difference between problem solving and obsessively overthinking and it looks as follows:

- **Overthinking**: 'Jenny hasn't replied to my birthday dinner invitation. I need to know if she is coming because there is only a certain amount of space. If Jenny can't come there will be a spare seat at the table and then I will have to pay for this and I already didn't invite Katie. Maybe Jenny hasn't replied because I said something to upset her. What did I say to her when we last spoke? I didn't invite her to lunch with me and Gemma last month, I wonder if she heard this and now thinks I'm rude. My birthday dinner is going be ruined. It's going to end up being awkward because Jenny isn't coming and everyone will wonder why. I wonder if I should just cancel the whole thing.'
- **Problem solving**: 'Jenny hasn't replied to my birthday dinner invitation. I need to know if she is coming because there is only a certain amount of space. I'll give Jenny a call and see if she is free. If she isn't, I could invite Katie, or see if anyone wants to bring someone as a plus one.'

Overthinking problems doesn't fix them, it just leaves us feeling exhausted by our spinning thoughts. So, at the end of this chapter, I'm going to offer up some ideas for how to tackle the negative side of overthinking.

However, before I do that, I want to point out the positive side to otherthinking, too. We started this chapter by referencing Einstein, one of the greatest minds to have ever existed. As mentioned, in his case, overthinking was linked to high achievement. This is the case for others too, especially in an academic setting, where it can be extremely powerful.

In a more general context, overthinkers can be introspective people, who are very self-aware. When harnessed in the right way, this can result in us having a growth mindset (an attitude of always continuing to learn and grow). Great news!

We overthinkers are also creative. A study at King's College in London concluded that those who think a lot have a high creative IQ. Essentially, us overthinkers are imaginative souls who can foresee many different outcomes.

Those who overthink may also be great at planning and to-do lists. We are ready for almost every eventuality. You can't surprise the overthinker because we've already thought of it, both the positive and, most definitely, the negative outcomes.

Finally, obsessive overthinkers can be very passionate and dedicated people who see the bigger picture and the finer details. We are always looking for answers and this can take us on some really fun adventures in our pursuit of them.

You see, the overthinking that at times may drive you nuts is in fact also a superpower that, when channelled in a positive way, can propel you into brilliance.

I'm feeling better about my overthinking, but it's still annoying, what can I do?

1 **Be aware of ANTs**. No, not the cheeky ones that made a nice home by my back door last year and had to be coaxed out with sugary treats. I mean Automatic Negative Thoughts. It is said that those who

overthink have high reactivity in the amygdala. This is the area of the brain that responds to threat, which means that those who overthink tend to be quick to perceive something as a threat. Start to become aware of when the overthinking happens most. What's the trigger? And when do you know it's a good time to overthink? This awareness can allow you to be ready to tackle it head-on, or use it to your advantage.

2 **Get your pen and paper out**. In moments of an overthinking frenzy, write down your thoughts. Get them out and then work out what emotion connects them all. Let's say it's fear. You would then consider what the fear is and write a sentence to state this: 'I feel scared I won't get a good job.' When the overthinking begins you can then say to yourself: 'These thoughts are fears that I won't get another job.' And then ask: 'What actions can I take to help myself with this?'

3 **Take action**. Overthinking keeps us firmly in our thinking brain and less in our doing. To counteract this, I want you to *do* something. Let's continue with the example of wondering if you'll ever get that new job. Your overthinking brain can ponder on this all day and, before you know it, you're spiralling out of control. Instead, *do something*. Perhaps that's creating a new CV, getting references, looking at the jobs out there or listing what you would need to be in that role.

4 **Wake up your senses**. Let's get out of your head and into the now by shocking the senses. Go outside, spray your favourite fragrance, splash water on your face, do 10 star jumps. In fact, moving and doing some form of exercise has such enormous benefits to your mental health and in physically refocussing our minds. Shaking yourself out of the thinking by activating your senses can help you gain perspective and takes your brain to what you're doing in that moment.

'Overthinking can propel you into brilliance.'

#40

We're all going to die!

When you bought this book, I imagine the 'happy' in the title meant you assumed we wouldn't be discussing death, but alas this is not the case.

We are all going to die and the more comfortable we can be with this fact, the more alive we can be while we live.

Having been at both births and a death, I can say that both aspects of our human existence are inspiring. It sounds so weird to find a death inspiring, but I believe it can be (if we make a decision to view it this way). Being at my husband's death created within me a deep desire to live, and to live in a way that soaks up everything and appreciates my 'gift' of being alive.

'To live is the rarest thing in the world. Most people just exist, that is all.' This is one of my favourite Oscar Wilde quotations, and reminds me that I don't want to just plod through life and experience none of it.

There is no doubt that discussing death is terrifying for many because talking about it means we have to face the fact that we have a shelf life, and that is scary. But the avoidance of conversations about death means that many of us miss the power of focusing on the end (NB: I know that many people believe in an afterlife or many afterlives, but don't worry, that still sits side by side with what I'm saying – in 'this' version of life, there is an end, even if you believe there is more to come).

Have you ever had to hand in a piece of work by a certain deadline? I guarantee that having the deadline has made you work harder, dig deeper and get on with it. How about we begin seeing our lives as having a deadline and noticing how our priorities change.

The question 'What would you do if this were your last day on earth?' has always irked me, mostly because the answers people give are often far-fetched and clichéd. When I've heard people answer in the past, they've always opted for wild things, such as diving out of a plane or jetting off somewhere exotic to do crazy activities they'd never normally try if they had to live with the consequences.

My answer would be rather mundane. I'd gather around my loved ones and probably just chat and eat good food. If I only had one more day then there wouldn't be a great deal of time left, but for most of you reading this you'll have many more days and so there *is* time to give it a bit more consideration.

So, how do we approach this? Let's imagine you have died. What legacy would you like to have left? When people talk about you and who you were, what would you like them to say? What mark would you like to leave on this world? It might be something simple, as was the case for my husband Ross, who said, 'Just tell them I'm a good bloke, tell them I was all right.'

Considering these legacy questions can help you to lead a more purposeful life, and having a purpose is a hugely important factor when it comes to our happiness. I know purpose is a very grand notion, so don't get caught up in this too much. If the end goal, for example, is to leave a legacy of kindness, then think about what you have to do to achieve this.

If we go back to the idea of having a deadline, one of the really brilliant consequences of thinking like this is that you can start shedding aspects of your life that truly aren't important in the grand scheme of things. What are the things that don't add to your life, aren't needed and may even be holding you back? If you were going to die imminently, what would you stop worrying about?

Maybe it'd be keeping up appearances and competing with everyone around you? Or the worry that you're not good enough or that you've put on a few pounds? Perhaps you would stop telling yourself you can't and begin giving more things a go. I believe there would be many things that'd have far lower priority than you're giving them right now.

Impermanence can also be a very freeing notion. If you know that eventually we won't be around then does it really matter if you look silly once in a while or mess up a little (or a lot)? Reframing our lives in this way can help us gain some perspective and stop taking everything so seriously.

Your life is important and you have important stuff to do. Even if you feel like a tiny speck on the planet, it's amazing the impact one human can have by just putting out a little good into the world. The ripple effect of this can continue for many years after they have died.

The long and short of it is that our life has a use-by date. Acknowledging this and looking death in the eyes can be the trigger that encourages you to do all the things you want to, and to stop doing all the things you don't.

I'm going to die, so how can I make sure I'm alive now?

1 **Fast-forward to the end of your life and write a 'look back on my life' journal entry.** Write it in the present tense and reflect on all the wonderful things you hope you'll have done, and how you would like people to think about you when you're gone.

2 **Ask yourself regularly: 'Would I care about this if I was going to die tomorrow?'** On the days when you're worrying for hours about what colour scheme you should have for your 40th birthday party, or whether your boss actually likes you or not, ask yourself this question and watch how laughable many of your daily worries become.

3 **Instantly write down 10 things that bring you joy** or that you would like to have more of in your life. Don't judge this. Don't overcomplicate it and don't work out how, just use the sense of urgency from this chapter to admit and acknowledge what you want; the how can come later.

4 **Reflect and appreciate**. Death will enter all of our lives at some point, whether through the death of a loved one or seeing a friend grieving. Rather than always skipping past these moments as fearful and tragic, take a moment to reflect on your own life. Gain perspective about what matters, clarity about what you want next and a deep appreciation of being alive.

'Be alive, while you *are* alive.'

#41

Be nice

In 2004, I spent a day doing press interviews at my record label's head office. One of the interviews was with a big UK newspaper that was considered more highbrow than the tabloid ones I'd given interviews for earlier. The interviewer arrived as I was eating lunch and as he stepped into the room I jumped up, shook his hand and stopped eating my food. I'd always been taught not to talk with my mouth full and I didn't want to chat with bits of bread and soup spraying out at the journalist.

We did the interview and it seemed to go pretty well. When the article came out it was a double-page spread and was seen as a big deal by my management company to have secured it.

My style at the time (which I admit was very much curated by the record label) was the pop rock vibe we saw the likes of Avril Lavigne sporting. Pop with a gentle edge. At that time in my life I was savvy but still fairly unsure of myself in the 'big smoke' of London and still trying to find my own voice.

The article, although still seen as a success by the record label, talked about me having (and I'm paraphrasing) 'no rock attitude' and that I was so nice I stopped eating my food to chat. At the time, I felt really embarrassed about the article and a sense of shame about the 'nice girl' tag. I thought perhaps I should have 'performed' and smashed up a TV to create a more rock and roll image.

The snarky article left me with the story that being 'too nice' got you nowhere and, although thankfully I didn't let it bother me too much and have since recognised that idea is total BS, it's definitely a belief that prevails in some areas of society.

'Nice guys finish last' and the feeling that being kind is a weakness is something I want to stamp out.

In 2020, the gorgeous and talented presenter Caroline Flack committed suicide and her fans went into shock. We felt we knew her – she could have been our friend, a neighbour, a sister, and many in the UK in particular mourned her loss. During this time there was a public outcry about how Caroline had been treated by people on social media and in the mainstream press. People began posting 'Just be nice!' and 'If you've nothing nice to say, then don't say anything' across their social media feeds and I spoke on various radio shows about my own anger at the abuse Caroline had received. Caroline's story highlights the importance of embracing 'nice'.

Helping people is extremely important in my work; it's the reason I wrote this book and it makes me feel good. The Dalai Lama calls this phenomenon 'selfish altruism' and it is often referred to as a 'helper high'. Simply put, I help you, you feel good, and you feeling good means I feel good. What a wonderful ripple effect of kindness. Plus, it's steeped in some real science to back it up, which shows that being nice lowers stress and makes us happier.

For this reason, I often take time to respond to people via my social media streams. People come to me with worries about having to hand in their notice, stand up and do a presentation at work or how to deal with their grief or pain, and I try my very best to respond to these because the saying 'never leave a man behind' lives in my head and motivates me to help. When I get feedback that I have helped someone through a difficult time I feel good, it warms my heart. Being nice is win–win.

I know you're here because you want to feel happy, and being nice to others is a sneaky shortcut to your own happiness, so give it a go.

I want to be nice AF, how can I spread the love?

1 **Perform random acts of kindness (RAK)**. This is a term that has become popular over the last few years. It means doing something lovely for someone with no expectation of getting anything in return. Buy someone a coffee, make someone some food and drop it off at their house, send someone some flowers, clean a neighbour's car or take their wheelie bin out (like my wonderful neighbour Rachel does for me, way more than she probably wants to – thanks Rach!). These gestures don't have to cost money to have impact, so give RAK a go.

2 **Compliment people**. Be really specific in your complimenting. Make it genuine and surprising. Compliment someone's parenting (high five the mum who just dealt with a tantrum in the supermarket), compliment someone's handwriting or sense of style. Compliment a friend who just launched her business and the amazing website she has put together. Compliment someone for being nice.

3 **Support people**. Life is tough at times and we all need a little help now and then. Be the supporter and cheerleader of others (and on a selfish note, I promise you'll get it back!). When you buy from a local business, make sure you review them and shout about their work on social media. Comment on the girl from school's Facebook post where she sells personalised champagne flutes and like her business page too. Offer up your babysitting services to family members. As a mum, I know how much this can be needed now and then. Champion those around you and support them in any way you can. Being nice will always come back to you.

‹Being nice is badass!›

#42

Making friends with fear

'If you're not scared, you're not paying attention' was a line I heard on TV recently and it made me chuckle.

It's so true.

As we emerge from our quilt covers and prise open our eyes, we look around our bedrooms and our thoughts instantly spring into action. 'You need to have that super important meeting with your boss today. Are you prepared? Have you done a good enough presentation? Maybe she'll fire you?'

'You still haven't called Aunt Megan to let her know you won't be attending her birthday party. She's probably going to be upset with you and think you're so rude.'

'You promised yourself you were going to start taking ice cold showers every day, like that girl on Pinterest said you should. That means you need to get up now and honestly it's going to be awful, I hear some people nearly pass out the first time!'

And the fear kicks in.

Fear is a normal human reaction and our brain's way of trying to survive. The moment we feel unsafe or unsure, our brain thinks, 'You know, I don't know how I feel about this situation and I think retreat may be the best option until I have more information.' It's pretty smart really.

I mean, if we didn't have *any* fear, none at all, we would be in a world of trouble. This would see us hugging lions, walking too close to the edge of cliffs and putting our hands into flames (none of which are recommended pastimes). Fear is an emotion with a very important function as it keeps us safe, so in this chapter I'm certainly not advocating that we erase all fear completely. I am, however, making sure we aren't so fearful that we cannot leave the house and perhaps miss out on exciting opportunities.

When I think about the times in my own life when I have been scared, they rank on a scale of varying degrees of importance and severity. For example, when I was pregnant for the first time with my daughter Brooke, and I knew motherhood was imminent (although I definitely didn't anticipate her premature arrival), I was scared. I didn't know how to be a mum and I'd never been the one to hold other people's babies and coo over them. This was mild fear, though, because I had a level of trust that I would just work it out.

When I was told by a surgeon that he anticipated my husband had a maximum of 15 weeks left to live, however, the fear hit me like a train. It was like a physical punch in the gut and I could barely breathe. *This* fear spun me out into an unknown future and my brain went into a frenzy.

Thankfully, prior to these occurences of major life and death-type fears, I had become quite hardened to fear, having practised putting myself in situations that were nerve-wracking. This helped to reduce my recovery time after I received the major fear-inducing news and meant I recognised I simply had to face my fear in order to walk myself towards feeling safe again.

Let's put this into context in your own life. Let's say your current fear is the presentation you have to do at work next month or the first dance at your wedding. How can you help yourself to do these things and manage the fear? Prepare, plan and practise are a great trio of actions to start with. You could do mock versions of both of these events, and perhaps perform them to a trusted person first so you can build up to the real event.

When we do things that feel scary at first and accomplish them (whatever they may be), we train our brain that we *can* and then when we face the big gut-wrenching fearful moments, we can tap into our now well-practised habit of facing our fears head-on.

Every day there is room for fear, and there is also room for choice. You may have got into the habit of taking the easy route, to silence your fear brain, staying firmly in your comfort zone and rarely venturing out. No judgement, it makes sense, but in order for us to make sure you don't miss out on some amazing opportunities in life you need to find ways to jump into the unknown and push past the fear.

I'm scared of lots of stuff, what can I do?

1 **Stop feeding the fear**. The fears you have come from something you heard, saw or experienced previously. So, perhaps it's now time to look at where the fears originate from and check in to see if you are still exposing yourself to similar conversations, people or situations that are exacerbating what you're feeling. Let's say you have a fear of being judged, and your current friendship group spend most of their time gossiping about and judging others. This environment will most definitely feed your fear of stepping out of what is 'acceptable' in your current circle and limit some of your choices.

2 **Make fear your friend**. If you feel nervous or a bit fearful, this often means you're pushing yourself out of your comfort zone. Once we stop seeing fear as the enemy, we can start to recognise its power. Fear is the friend who will check to see whether you're

on the right track and if the choices you're making have positive consequences. This doesn't mean fear has all the answers – it doesn't, because we often have to take a leap before we have all the information – but at the very least it will make you stop and really consider your course of action.

3 **Steer the fear**. Knowing when to push through the fear is important and it largely comes down to the question: 'If I push through this fear, will the action I take bring me closer to the life I want or further away?' For example, you may be scared to attend a job interview, but if this is a job you want, pushing through the fear is essential. Since we will never eradicate fear, we have to have a reason to push through it. Creating a strong purpose or 'why' for doing the thing we are scared of can help us to be a little brave. We may still be shaking in our boots while we take the step, but knowing where we are heading and what we want to achieve will help us to feel courageous enough to keep trying.

4 **Imagine this**. You're old, in your bed, surrounded by loved ones and thinking back on your life. Will you be happy if the fears that you are carrying now stopped you doing the things you really want to do? Will you be in that bed feeling regretful or smiling as you remember what an adventure it's all been. If you can switch it up and make the fear of not doing the things you want to do stronger than the fear of actually just giving things a go, then you've cracked it.

"Every day there is room for fear and there is also room for a different choice."

#43

Comparison

Comparisonitis: *The art of obsessively comparing your life to someone else's life and making yourself feel miserable in the process.*

As an older millennial, I am lucky enough (and I actually believe it is lucky) to have lived my life both before the internet came along and with it. This allows me to have a clear perspective on the culture we have created online, which bits serve us and which bits really don't.

Pre internet, or should I say pre social media, we had limited access to information about what other people were doing. We had very little knowledge, for example, about what breakfast our neighbour was eating or whether the woman from the gym had a new outfit of the day (OOTD). We didn't know what people bought their children for Christmas (or how much!) and we had to actually visit people to see their newly decorated kitchen.

These days, we wake from our possibly rather restless sleep (having also been scrolling before bed) to pick up our phones and dive straight into the perfectly polished version of some stranger on the internet's life. I hold my hands up and admit I am guilty of endless scrolling and I can't pass any judgement on this modern pastime. But when I put it like that, it sounds rather ridiculous, doesn't it?

The thing is, while endlessly perusing other people's lives, we often find ourselves comparing our lives to theirs. 'Come on Holly!' (I hear you cry) 'We've been doing this since time began. It's normal and part of human nature.' I agree, it is, but the problem with comparing your life to those you see online is that it is not a fair comparison. It's not a fair fight.

Ask yourself what *you* share on social media. Is it the argument you had with your boyfriend last night? When you called him an idiot and said you hate his favourite shoes? That time you got drunk on your friend's hen do and cried the whole evening? Do you share the big fat pile of ironing that is leaning against the patchy wall you've been meaning to paint since you moved into your house … four years ago?

Gosh, I imagine your feed is full to the brim of pictures you've taken the moment you wake, with a brand-new spot on your face, sleep in your eyes and messy hair?

Oh, sorry, it's not? Well, what a shocker!

Of course, it isn't. No ones does this. Everyone posts the version of their lives that they want the world to see. They post the best bits, the showy bits, the sparkly bits and the bits you secretly hope everyone is going to envy.

That, my friends, is the world of social media and it ain't going nowhere. Plus, it's not just confined to social media. Perhaps you've been comparing yourself to someone at work who seems like they have everything together, or the girl in the year above you at school who you heard from your aunty has some super important corporate job in London. The comparisons can be endless.

The problem with it though is that we compare our crappy bits to the very best bits of other people's lives, and then wonder why we don't feel all that great about ours.

You *know* your awful moments, your embarrassing stuff, and you have zero idea of anyone else's. Even if they look polished to perfection, you're not a mind reader and they're only showing you the section of their lives that they want you to see.

Let me tell you my own real-life reality check about comparison.

Here I am back in 2010, a TV actress, things are on the up and I get the exciting news that I'm pregnant with my first daughter. It's a lovely surprise and I am thrilled. I had been planning to head out to America with my husband to do the casting circuit in January, but since I'm now pregnant I decide to wait.

At the same time, a girl I know, who is a fashion model, has flown over to work and study out there. I am friends with her on Facebook and keep an eagle eye on her progress.

Here I am, getting steadily fatter in cold and grey Coventry, turning down acting parts due to my growing bump and watching Model Girl doing yoga on an LA beach: tanned, slim, gorgeous, getting acting parts and attending celeb parties.

The green-eyed monster is up and WIDE awake. I am on a comparison rampage and eventually (because I practise what I preach) I unfollow her.

About a year later, the same girl contacts me and asks me to be her coach. While I had been salivating over her life, she had been doing the same to me. Unbeknownst to me, she was sad, lonely, missing home, desperate to have children ... and starving!

I had imposed the ideal version of her life – not the very different reality – on to some photos on social media and compared my own life to that. I took this as the universe giving me a wake-up call and showing me how pointless this behaviour was. (Head to 'Spilling the tea on fake social media lives' on p. 92 for more on this.)

There's probably some truth in the fact that during this comparison 'frenzy' I was doing less with my time, so I had more time to focus outside of myself. When we are consuming but not creating things for ourselves it can leave us wide open to being self-critical. Whereas when my life is full of wonderful things to get excited about, I'm just not interested in obsessing over other people's lives.

If an idle brain seeks out things to compare our lives to, and then chastises us for not living up to someone else, then it's important to bring some awareness to this fact, and consider further factors that might trigger our comparison brain. Begin noticing whether there's any correlation between what you're doing in your life or how you feel about yourself in that moment, and then as a result how much of others' lives you begin consuming.

It's also important you bring awareness to how you currently measure the comparison. What is wealth or success for example? Is it the trappings of socially approved success like money, jewellery and houses, or is it the wealth my Grandma Rita enjoys? Grandma 'Wilkie' is surrounded by people who love and adore her. She has a cosy home that she has decorated as she likes, her lovely dog Toby and years of wonderful memories and legacy. There are many ways to measure success, health, wealth and beauty and by just changing the way we quantify them, we might find we have way more than those we are comparing ourselves to.

'Comparison is the thief of joy' as they say and probably the thief of time, too, seeing that we spend so much of ours doing it.

So how do we stop comparing ourselves to others, whether on social media or in real life? Because believe me, it's a habit we really need to break in order to feel good. Let's take a look.

What to do today, like right now!

1 **Remind yourself that there is only one of you**. No one can be a better version of you than you. When you try to be someone else, you only ever become a rubbish version of that person, when you could be being the best version of yourself. You can't be me and I can't be you, so trying to is a waste of our time.

2 **Unfollow every social media account that makes you feel envy**. Social media should be a place to inspire and connect, not to make you feel bad.

3 **Remember that you are only seeing a snapshot of a person's best bits** and you have no idea if a perfect Insta couple just had a row about the woman from work, or if behind that perfectly positioned avocado breakfast is a kitchen that looks like a bomb went off.

4 **Know that while you are focusing on other people, you are *not* focusing on how you can live your best life**. So spend less time looking at the girl from work's wedding snaps (from two years ago!) and more time smashing your own life goals. Comparison is merely wasting your time and distracting you from all the great things you could be doing with your own life.

5 **Use other people's success as inspiration, not a source of envy**. Rather than pining after someone else's achievements and doing the whole 'I'm not where they are/where I should be/as good as them' thing, turn it round and recognise that if they can achieve what they have, then this means there's an audience and space for you to do it, too. Someone else's success does not diminish your ability to succeed.

6 **Focus on your best bits**. What are *you* good at? If you just said 'nothing' in your head then I'm going to march over to your house and get real stern with you! You *are* good at stuff. Are you a good friend? A good listener? A bloody fantastic dancer? A budding chef? There is something sincerely wonderful about you and *that* is what your time should be spent focused on.

‹There's no better you than you, and when you compare yourself to others you water down your magic.›

#44

Love hard

I got married at the age of nine. To Robbie Williams from Take That. It was 1993 and I wore a pillow case on my head as a veil while my friends Eve and Bryony played the vicar and threw confetti on me. I loved him.

Little wonder then that it blew my mind a few years ago when my friend Brian interviewed Robbie for his YouTube channel 'True Geordie', and I was informed that Robbie had watched my own interview with Brian.

Although my 'love' for Robbie has diminished ever so slightly over the years, it's important to reflect on all the things and people we have loved as we look to bring more love and joy into our current lives. I don't just mean romantic love, either. I mean the love of a mother and her daughter, the man and his dog, and the things in our daily life that we love to see, do, hear, eat and binge watch on Amazon Prime.

The cliché says that love makes the world go round and I fully buy into this concept. It might sound very New Age and hippie, but in big picture terms, love is needed for our survival because without the pull of love we don't have connection and without connection we will not procreate. Also, when we are loved and love, our bodies produce a big heap of the hormone oxytocin, which helps us to feel happy and joyful. Therefore, on a scientific level, love has been proven to lower our stress levels and even benefit our heart health.

The world is not set up to help us be in a space of love, though. Every day we are bombarded with things to hate and dislike. Whether it's the obnoxious images of people abusing their power or the environment, or the grim scenes of hate at anti-LGBTQ+ rallies. Everyday acts of racism, sexism, greed, selfishness, hate and lack of tolerance are smeared across our screens and jump out at us on our news feeds.

When we allow hate to permeate our lives, it eats away at us like a virus and our brain keeps seeking out more of the same (as we discussed in 'How the brain works' on p. 16). We begin to see negativity in everything, as our brains learn to seek out the bad and overlook the good. Even the most well-rounded of us can easily pick up the bad habit of letting too much angst into our little worlds, and begin to forget what is really important...

Love.

Love has the power to break down barriers and cross divides, it will pick us up when we've lost all hope and knock us off our feet when we least expect it.

When we change our attitude and actively seek more things to love, we begin to see the world in a new light. Our expectation of attracting love allows us to spot more things to love. It's like a light switch is turned on and we can see the magical, joyful things around us.

Expressing our love for things and people has a ripple effect too. I constantly tell my children I love them and, specifically, *what* I love about them. This makes them feel loved and they in turn tell others the same, compliment people and talk about the things they love. I regularly declare my love for sunsets and the little robin that lands in my garden. I take endless photos of things I love and have actually stopped my car to photograph a really pretty plant that was growing on a fence at the end of my street (I know this one is a bit weird, I knew it as I did it).

I love hard. I am a hopeless romantic and adore hearing how people fell madly in love. I like it when people share photos of their babies and their pets and, most especially, their love for themselves. I used to think this was a bit too much and would judge these public expressions of love harshly. However, after my husband died, I realised that loves can be taken in a moment and that is why appreciating the things we love now is so important.

So my message to you is this: Love with all your heart. Then, even if that love dies out or you're no longer able to love that person or thing any more, you will know that for that time in your life there was joy.

Don't taint your joy of something or someone with worries about what someone else will think. Life is too short for that nonsense and you deserve your world to be drenched in love. Not everyone will understand the reason you love what and who you do, and that's OK. When we send out love into the world, life is happier and more colourful.

I want more love, how can I bring it into my world?

1 **Gush about it!** Talk openly about the things you love, every day. Share this love with those around you, on social media and to anyone who will listen. Talk about the things you love and see more things to love appear. Perhaps you could take photos of things you love. When you do this regularly, you will create a visual record of love. On days when things are tough, you can scroll through these and top yourself back up with happiness.

2 **'Bank' your moments of love.** When you have moments of love, be it a kiss with your daughter, a hug with your grandma or laughing heartily at TikTok videos with your bestie, for a moment just notice and 'bank' the moment. This simply means taking a mental snapshot of the interaction and how you feel, which you can look back on at a later date to remind yourself of the good times.

3 **Tell people you love them**. It's easy to forget, but tell those you love that you love them, let people know you appreciate their existence on this planet and that they are important. Go on, text them, call them, tag them in a post or walk into the room they're in and declare your love. You never know who needs to hear it.

4 **Be compassionate**. Remember that everyone is struggling with something in their life and are doing the best they can. Find understanding and compassion, even for those who think differently from you. By doing this, you are also showing compassion to yourself and will in turn attract back compassion from others.

'Love will break down barriers and cross divides. It will pick us up when we've lost all hope and knock us off our feet when we least expect it.'

#45

Make trouble – break the rules

From the second we're born we are being taught rules and ways to behave. We head to school and want to fit in, to please our teachers or parents, and over time this means we slowly start to conform. We become obedient and silenced and sometimes, without us noticing, we begin to hide our true selves.

I'm lucky in that although my parents had regular jobs (my dad was a welder and my mum worked in a bank), they didn't conform to the norm. They had been punks and always taught me and my sister, Beki, to express ourselves and live our truth. As a parent myself now, I want my girls to question everything (even me, which can be highly annoying!) and I want them to push boundaries.

I have a wish that extends to my clients and to *you* too: I want you to recognise that some rules are merely a guide and that you, on a personal level, don't have to do what everyone else is doing, just because it seems like the way you *should* be behaving. (Please note I did say *some* not *all* rules here – we don't want you breaking the law!)

We get so worried that if we step out of line we will be judged, or appear weird, that we often fight what instinctively feels right to us. Look at marriage, for example. The pressure put on people to conform to the traditional weddings of each culture is enormous. I have had friends cry to me about the stress they've felt while organising a wedding that wasn't even what they wanted – they were doing it a certain way to suit those around them.

I personally never fancied the traditional method of getting married and neither did my parents, who got married unconventionally (my mum sported bright red hair and a wedding dress and my dad wore a zoot suit with yellow shoes). This meant that I already understood that some rules are meant to be broken.

I got married without telling anyone, grabbing a couple of work acquaintances (who then became very close friends) as witnesses, and wearing a hoody and trainers, while my husband wore a football shirt. Afterwards, we went for a cup of tea and a cake. Very British.

Were my family happy? Not really. Did I want to upset them? Of course not. Are they OK about it now? Of course they are, and it's probably a very fun story for them to share with friends.

If you want a life you have created to fit *your* needs, you are going to have to break a few rules. Now I am not suggesting, when I say break the rules, that you start breaking the law and running amuck, as I've already clarified. I am talking about breaking social constructs. These are rules that we as a society collectively just follow, that we consciously or subconsciously accept as how things are done.

Rules are often created to control and limit you; they're about keeping things in order and not rocking the boat. So, in order to create anything different you have to step outside these lines and work out the path that suits you.

Happiness is not a one-size-fits-all deal. How I find happiness will be different to how you find happiness, and so staying within a template that others have set out for you and expecting to find your happy life is crazy. The happiest people in the world are those who are sometimes seen as rebels, visionaries and rule breakers. They're the people who speak their mind, who live their truth, who stand up and share their opinions, and who don't care if they're reprimanded for it.

When you finally decide to start being exactly who you want to be it will feel liberating, like a weight has been lifted from your shoulders, and everything will just feel easier. However, here's my warning: at times it will get a little uncomfortable and some people are going to have something to say about it. People will wag their fingers, gossip, judge and do all the stuff that has kept you from having lived your truth up until this point. When this happens, which it will, you are going to need to dig deeper than ever before. You're going to need to remind yourself *why* what you're doing is important to you and you're going to have to turn on your blinkers and stay in your own lane.

Just after I got married, someone I care about said, 'You'll regret getting married in that way, it just isn't as special', and at the time it stung.

Do I regret it?

Absolutely not. It was exactly what I wanted at the time, it was fun, it summed us up as a couple and it's a great story. I can sit comfortably knowing that no matter how uncomfortable or perhaps disappointed other people were about that decision, for the two people involved, whose marriage it was, we were happy, and surely *that's* the point.

How to become a kick-ass rule-breaking legend!

1 **Ask yourself some fundamental questions**. It's helpful to reflect on your life as it stands now, so that you can see where there may be areas in which you've become stuck or where there may be room to switch things up. Ask yourself:

- When have you ever broken the rules or gone against the grain?
- What rules are you following now and how is this helping you?
- Who gave you the rules to follow?
- What would happen if you broke some rules?

2 **Speak your mind**. Your voice matters, your opinions matter, we need to hear you. As you go through your day, I want you to actively voice your opinion, perhaps even disagree to see what it feels like (I know sometimes it can be tempting to go with the group) – be a little brave and get off the fence. Start small as always. For example, perhaps instead of agreeing that you enjoyed *Game of Thrones* (because everyone else seemed to), confidently admit you found it boring. Or maybe you step it up a little further and challenge grandad about his outdated opinions on women or argue the case for pineapple on pizza. You won't be alone in your opinion, even if you are in that one moment, and it will feel great to get it off your chest.

3 **Do something that you believe in**. Decide to only buy from sustainable fashion brands, stop buying stuff you don't need, quit sugar (you'd be a bigger person than me if you do!), fight against social injustice or volunteer to help at an animal sanctuary. Or perhaps none of these things matter to you – in which case choose something different. You decide how to spend your time by going with your heart rather than by following the social norm. This is your life, no one else's, so create your own rules and live by them.

"Some of the happiest people in the world are those who are sometimes seen as rebels, visionaries and rule breakers."

#46

You're not running out of time

Do you know what really gets on my nerves? When people say, 'We all have the same hours in the day as Beyoncé.' Like this is supposed to make us spring into action and go, 'Yeah, you're right! I mean, of course, I don't have the team of people around me to get me dressed, do my hair and organise my day like she does, but sure I have the same hours in the day as Beyoncé, so let me get stuff done.'

I personally find that sort of rhetoric demotivating, as it can slip me into procrastination mode and then make me worry I'm running out of time. Just so you can get a really clear picture of what this looks like, imagine me sitting in my comfy clothes, doing nothing, probably holding a cup of tea, looking like a zoned-out zombie, panicking that 'time is running out'. The irony of this is not wasted on me.

The feeling of time slipping away has always been there. I remember that at the age of 16 I worried that time was against me because I wasn't in a Hollywood movie yet and very soon I would be 18 and essentially over the hill. At 20, I went to drama school and I felt so old compared to those young whippersnappers straight out of college. So I think that for me and many others, this is a problem whatever your age. We constantly think we are missing the boat and not doing things quickly enough.

Like all anxiety-based thoughts, when you dig under the surface you might find a common set of behaviours happening. I'm extremely rigid when it comes to time in general. I organise my time, I'm never late and even if I create a schedule and the consequences of me changing it are really small, I still feel a level of anxiety when this happens. Sticking on my detective hat and exploring what was really happening meant I realised that my biggest concern is actually that I don't want to 'waste' my time and I want to have a sense of meaning in my life.

I am well aware that I am not the only person who feels this panic about the 'shoulds'. The 'I *should* be successful by now.' 'I *should* have found the man of my dreams by now.' 'I *should* have had children by now.' Insert your own 'should' here because I know you can relate, so let's work through it and quiet the noise.

Feeling like your time is running out is awful. We all know time is not infinite, so the urgency remains in the background even when we rationalise it. This can lead to us hurrying unnecessarily and not appreciating the right now. The pace of the world can be fast, and in addition we see people who seemingly have it all and do it all put on a pedestal, which doesn't help.

When we don't hit the life milestones in the order society tells us we should, we instinctively feel like we messed up. This thought process sends us into comparison mode and makes us feel like we're lacking and not good enough. (*See* 'Comparison' on p. 186 for more on this.)

I think the truth to this time anxiety is that we aren't worried about time moving forwards, we're just worried about wasting the time we have on things that just don't feel important to us. The key to taking hold of this seems to be organising the time you have in a way that allows space for you to be doing things that are of high value to you. Being aware enough of the things you want in life and then making space for them so you can look back and think, 'Yep, I did what I came here to do and I feel great about how I spent my time.' You can read 'We're all going to die!' on p. 174 to help you decide what you really value in life, right now.

The pace of your life and the order you do it in does not equate to the quality of your life and your happiness. Instead of saying things like 'I am so annoyed I left this so late', try saying, 'I am so glad I now get to experience this.' The timeline of how you do things is for you and only you to decide.

I feel like I've missed the boat, what can I do?

1 **Be present**. This moment is all that is real. You look ahead and it's guesswork, you look behind and it's already gone. The more you can be present and in this moment, the less you will worry about what you 'should' have done. Take a moment right now to breathe in a nice full breath (yes, right now), look around the room and acknowledge where you are. What can you hear, smell, taste, feel and see? Rub your hands together and feel the heat you generate in the friction. Drop your shoulders and unclench your jaw. Wake yourself up to *this* moment and slow down to speed up. Check out 'Mindful AF' on p. 136 for more tips.

2 **Stop saying 'I'm running out of time' or 'it's too late'**. Change the language you use to create the reality you want: 'I have all the time I need' and 'The order I do things in is the right order for me'.

3 **Look at your life and where your time is being spent**. Where are the time saps? It's often worth actually timing yourself as you do things to see how long they really take. For example, I know I can do my make-up in 6–7 minutes if I just get on with it, but so often it takes me 45 minutes because I'm faffing. This is a time sap. Scrolling through social media is the king of time wasting and definitely also brings with it a bout of guilt. How can you get some 'scroll control' and limit the amount of time you lose?

4 **Factor in time for things that bring you a sense of 'meaning'** and that you believe add value to the world. Whether that's spending time playing with your children, getting enough exercise on a daily basis or working hard on a particular project in your professional life, if it brings you closer to the things that are core values to you, then it needs to be scheduled into your week. The more you feel you're adding something meaningful and good into the world, the less stressed you will feel when your timings get shifted around.

'Make time for stuff that matters.'

#47

Is this a good idea?

Don't do it.

Don't!

You did it, didn't you?

Our lives are shaped by the daily decisions that we take, the going left or the going right, the saying 'yes' or the saying 'no'. The big decisions, the small ones and the ones we really don't want to have to make.

We sometimes hear people utter the phrase 'everything happens for a reason' and I guess that sounds great on a fancy notepad or as a wall sticker for your teenage daughter's bedroom, but as fully grown adults, we have to finish that sentence: 'Everything happens for a reason and sometimes that reason is we made a really bad choice.'

Ouch. I know, it hurts when we remember we're human and don't always get it right. Life is a minefield and at every turn there is another thing we have to decide to do or not do, and if you're anything like me, there are days when you would happily opt out.

When we are little, our parents take over the choices and decide what we eat, wear and even who we hang out with. We might not like their choices at the time, but most parents are doing their very best to see the bigger picture and make decisions that they hope will help us to have a great life.

I try to explain this concept to my two daughters when I'm 'making' them do something, and of course it falls on deaf ears. So, recently, I challenged this form of parenting and allowed my eldest daughter to do something she wanted to do that I disagreed with.

Picture the scene: my daughter corners me as I'm about to get into the shower. 'Mum, I want to cut my own hair.' My instant parent reaction is 'Absolutely not.' The begging ensues and she begins to tell me all the reasons why she *should* be allowed. As she launches head first into a powerful monologue about 'trust' and this being 'her life', I quietly weigh up the situation.

What's the worst that can happen? A bad haircut that will grow out.

What could be the best thing to come out of it? A lesson that Mum's life experience and wisdom should perhaps be listened to and, probably more importantly, the lesson that the decisions we make impact our lives.

I tell her that I think it is a bad decision to cut her own hair. I remind her that she is not a hairdresser and it's very hard to cut your own hair. I inform her I will allow her to cut her own hair as long as she has heard loud and clear that I don't think it's a smart move.

Off she skips with her sister in tow and as I shower I hear giggling and squeals of 'I have a fringe!' As you can probably imagine, a short time later she thumps into my room, a bowl of hair in hand, sobbing at the mullet she has just given herself.

Friends and family were horrified when I shared this 'hilarious' story with them and there was quite a lot of judgement of me. However, Brooke is totally fine; she has grown to love her 'tuft' and she's learned that decisions have consequences.

Now in this particular example no harm was done, but sometimes in life we make a decision that does cause us damage. The lustful decision to cheat on a partner, for example, or the rash decision to sell everything you own to start a business selling *Doctor Who* merchandise. Both of these choices may lead you along a path you want to avoid. Perhaps the affair leads to heartache and pain and the business lands you with financial insecurity.

Ultimately, we have to take responsibility for our decision-making. We certainly don't want to be scared of making 'risky' or bold decisions but it's important to always check in to make sure our decisions align with who we want to be and our values.

When it comes to our happiness, I certainly won't be advising on the nitty gritty of your personal life – our choices are ours and ours alone. But let me share some common factors that frequently lead to poor decision-making that in the long term can really impact how we feel, so you can do your best to avoid them:

- **Waiting for the 'right time'**. This simply means you'll never get started and possibly miss your chance altogether.
- **Living your life for others**. Doing things for others, dressing for others, being who someone else thinks you should be when you know in your heart it doesn't feel right. This type of people-pleasing behaviour is a surefire route to sadness.
- **Burying your head in the sand**. Pretending things aren't happening when they most definitely are.
- **Being scared to try in case you fail**. We have to fail to become good at something, end of story and case dismissed. By never giving something a go, you will miss so many incredible adventures and fail by default.
- **Having a short-term mindset** and giving up before you've given something a chance. I know we feel like we should have a six pack after eating quinoa salad for lunch and doing 20 minutes of cardio but everything takes time and we won't always see the results we want quickly.
- **Settling for the minimum**. This could be how you allow others to treat you, how you feel about your work, your sense of self or your standards. If you're always doing the bare minimum then you'll never see how fabulous you and your life could possibly be.

So now we've discussed the things to avoid let's look at some tips to help with positive decision-making.

There are so many choices, what can I do?

1 **Know your bigger picture**. When making big or small decisions, always refer back to the values that are most important to you and consider whether the choice you're making is taking you closer to or further away from these. (For more information on discovering your values, *see* 'What does your ideal life look like?' on p. 72.)

2 **Facts and feelings**. Before making a decision, gather all the factual information you can, then sit with yourself and tune into how you feel about the options. Feelings aren't irrelevant, they're very important, and as long as you place them next to the hard facts, you'll be heading in a good direction.

3 **Understand it's OK to not always get things right** and be kind to yourself when your decision-making leads you down a path that didn't work out. It's also important to be aware that sometimes we can make some great decisions but the outcome may still not pan out as we wish. Sometimes the outcome is out of our hands.

'Good decisions are made using facts *and* feelings.'

#48

Getting to know yourself

Who are you?

Today. Who are you in *this* moment?

It's a funny question to ask but getting to know the 'right now' version of you is the only way you will learn how to make yourself feel happy.

I always cringe a little when people talk about 'finding themselves'. It feels very New Age and hippy and the majority of people don't really know what it means. Me included. I'm of the opinion that we are different versions of ourselves at different points in our lives. I once heard someone describe this idea as us having different 'levels', almost like a computer game, whereby as we age, we go up a level. I love this description as it certainly turns the 'youth is best' rhetoric on its head.

As we go up our levels in life we bring with us wisdom, experience, lessons learned and understanding (or at least we'd hope that we do). At each new stage, we need different things because we change and we are probably excited by different things. I imagine that if you compare the you of 10 years ago with the you of today, there has been change in lots of areas of your life – possibly huge change. The 25-year-old you might have been more concerned with what you're going to wear on your night out, whereas 35-year-old you might put more importance on what schools your children will attend and getting a mortgage. So let's think about *you* right now.

What do you need? What excites you? What scares you? What would you love to do and haven't yet? How are you braver than before, or possibly even that bit more scared?

For some of you reading this, it may be the first time you've really considered the idea of getting to know yourself. When you do a little digging, you might find that not only do you not really know who you are but perhaps you discover that you actually behave and respond to life according to opinions you have acquired from other people.

I often see clients who have been in relationships since they were very young and have no idea what their own personal likes and dislikes are. For some, finding out is a very laborious process and at first they find it very hard to not look for the 'right' answers.

The truth is that the 'right' answers are whatever feels good to you and no one else can help you with that. You don't get a gold star for getting to know yourself, you just begin to make decisions based on your own internal compass that leads you towards a happier life. I see these personal discoveries as clues, little snippets of information that can help us to make better decisions, manage our triggers and arrange our lives in a way that accommodates all of who we are.

Are you an introvert or an extrovert? If you're an extrovert and know you get energised by being social then you can make sure you're getting your 'hit' of people. If the opposite is true then you might know that after having been around a lot of people you'll need to refill your cup by being alone with a book or going for a run.

How can you set up your life in a way that suits what excites you? Are you a person who loves nature or someone who thrives on the hustle and bustle of city living? Are you adventurous and excited by the idea of jumping out of a plane or someone who would prefer to sit by a lake and read poetry by Keats?

There really is no right or wrong answer here, it's merely a case of thinking about it and then acting accordingly. The more you embrace all facets of your personality, the more opportunities you will find to make your life spectacular.

I wanna work out who I am, where do I start?

1 **Describe yourself in three words**. Write down your biggest strengths and weaknesses. What scares you? What excites you? What makes you cry? When do you feel at your happiest? If you could click your fingers and be somewhere, where would you like to be? What is your favourite memory? You will find lots of question-type lists online and it's a fun exploratory exercise to answer some of these as a prompt to get to know yourself. Don't overthink, just see what you write down. This is for no one but you.

2 **Bucket list**. Write a list, as long as you can possibly make it, of all the things you would love to do. I recently found out about a place called Giraffe Manor in Kenya and it went straight on to my list. It's fun to do this exercise with those you love, too, so you can see if there is anything on there that you can do together. They don't all have to be super adventurous, either, just things you haven't done that you would like to do.

3 **The three whys**. This concept was originally developed by Sakichi Toyoda in the 1900s and, in this context, it's a great way to find your purpose or meaning, and begin to explore who you are a little further. So, you might think: 'I want to move somewhere hot, with sandy beaches.' You then ask yourself: 'Why do I want to go somewhere hot with sandy beaches?' Answer: 'I think it would give me peace of mind and be a lovely way to bring up my children.' Next why: 'Why do you think it would bring you peace of mind and be a lovely way to bring up your children?' Answer: 'Because my children and I

can be outdoors and spend more time together.' Last why: 'Why is it important to you to spend more time with your children?' Answer: 'To build strong, happy and calm relationships with them.' And suddenly you are learning more about what's really important to you. You can explore any area of your life or challenge with this technique.

4 **Observe others and yourself**. Do some people watching. Notice how people interact with one another, how they carry themselves and what makes them smile. Consider what stands out about them and how this is similar or different to you. There should be no judgement of yourself while performing this exercise, it's simply about becoming more aware and revealing new things about yourself and how you differ from those around you.

5 **Ground yourself**. Take moments out of your day during which you ground yourself in the moment and ask yourself these questions:

- What emotion do I feel right now?
- What do I need in this moment?

Whatever answers come up, let go of judgement and honour who you are and what you need. Practising this self-awareness regularly can help you to be your own best friend and allow the truest version of you to come through.

'You're a different you in every chapter of your life.'

#49

Guilt

Over the past week, how many things have you felt guilty about?

Cast your mind back to the things you've done and consider how many times you've felt bad about something. Did you order takeaway when your fridge was full? Did you watch an entire season of a TV show in one day, washed down with a fizzy drink and a pizza? Did you skip exercising in favour of scrolling social media?

We feel guilty *a lot*.

Whether it's because we have ignored the family WhatsApp group for a week, or that we let our kids play on their iPads for an eternity, guilt is hard to avoid.

Guilt does serve a purpose sometimes in that it can act as a compass to show us where we may have gone a little wrong, but it ceases to be useful if it's continually switched on. 'Mum guilt', for example, shows up for every mum I know, including me, and quite honestly it's a pretty constant feeling.

I have fairly high self-esteem overall and I do this 'personal development stuff' every day, yet mum guilt is my Achilles heel. I know I try hard to be a great mum, I love my daughters utterly, I come up with fun activities to do, and yet the moment my daughter says, 'Why don't you bake cakes like other mums do?' I feel rubbish.

We weren't born guilty: the feelings of guilt develop over time. Tiny moments during which we feel 'less than' or 'not good enough' begin to cling to us and shape how we respond to future situations.

If I consider my day yesterday as an example, then my 'sins' were:

- I ignored my alarm clock and got up a little later than I should have done.
- I ate a chocolate pancake for breakfast.
- I didn't do my yoga.
- I ignored a call from my mum because I was focused on some work.
- I didn't finish some writing I wanted to do.
- I didn't fold up and put away the laundry that has been on my clothes horse for two days.

I mean, just look at that list... Lock me up and throw away the key! Logically, when I look at my 'sin diary' I know there are perfectly good reasons for all of these (and it's OK for the reason to be 'because I wanted to', by the way). Yet so many of us fail to shake off the perpetual guilt that we should be doing more.

The reason for this is that feeling guilt and blaming ourselves for 'underperforming' in some way is often much easier than sitting with the perhaps less desirable feelings of helplessness or sadness. So we choose to blame ourselves for a myriad of things that we have no business feeling guilty about, because guilt and blame do at least leave us feeling like we are in control of something.

Much of our guilt comes from ideas we learned as children and our innate need to be liked. 'If I behave in this way, I'm the good girl' stays with us for a long time. In addition, there are social and societal pressures to behave in certain ways and when we feel we aren't measuring up to these we pile on guilt and shame. Perhaps we haven't hit a milestone we feel we should have, we haven't fulfilled a goal we said we would or maybe it's even the guilt of not being the way another person wants us to be. Add in the fact that we get to stare into other people's lives through our phones all day, and see everyone else seemingly winning at life (while we feel like we aren't hitting the mark), and it's a pretty potent mix.

Over time, this insidious guilt begins to erode our self-esteem and chips away at our confidence. If left unchecked, it may even go one step further and begin causing more deep-rooted levels of depression, anxiety and upset.

Ultimately, guilt equals suffering and while we embark on our journey of seeking more 'happy' in our lives, we have to start noticing where we can eliminate unnecessary suffering.

I'm weighed down with guilt, what should I do?

1 **Dig out the root of the guilt**. Do you feel guilty for not finishing everything on your plate because you were taught as a child that 'there are people starving in the world' every time you left a chicken drumstick? Noticing where this guilt comes from can be interesting and help to loosen its grip.

2 **Ask yourself if you did actually do something wrong**. If you did, apologise, rectify the mistake and move forwards. Guilt is sometimes there for a valid reason, so a little check-in can determine if action is needed. Did you forget to send that bit of work you said you would? Cancel the night out at the last minute for no real reason? Shout at your partner because you were exhausted? Maybe it's time to swallow your pride and say sorry. This doesn't mean you are a bad person, just human.

3 **Name the feeling**. When we feel guilt and unrest bubbling in us, recognise what it is specifically and name it. Say to yourself 'I am

feeling guilt' or more specifically 'I feel guilty because I didn't give my kids enough time with me today.' The act of naming what is going on can often bring it to the surface and wake us up to the nonsense of it. You can then add (after first checking you've not actually done anything to feel guilty for) 'I have done nothing wrong, I am human and I let go of this guilt.'

4 **Practise self-compassion**. None of us are 'getting it right' all of the time, and what does that phrase really mean anyway? If a friend told you their list of daily 'sins', how would you treat them? I imagine you'd almost laugh at most of their perceived misdemeanours, so I want you to start looking at your own list in the same way. OK, you ate two ice creams today? Make healthier choices tomorrow. You're doing your best and your messy best is perfect.

"You're doing your best and your messy best is perfect."

#50

Heavily meditated

If you google 'meditation' you will find images of ethereal-looking people sitting in the lotus position with sunsets glowing behind them. Pictures of beachside loveliness and levels of relaxation that seem far removed from ordinary life.

I get how unobtainable this can all seem, so I'm here to demystify meditation for you. I want to help you to see that meditation is brilliant, it just doesn't normally look anything like it does on Pinterest.

Meditation has many definitions depending on whom you speak to but ultimately it's the practice of slowing down the mind, focusing inwards and creating more awareness of self. (I know that still sounds vague, but in this chapter I'll give you lots of real-life examples.)

One particularly interesting study showed that the biggest observed effect in those who meditated was a decrease in beta waves, when their brains were looked at on a magnetic resonance imaging (MRI) scan. These beta waves indicate that our brain is processing information, and those who meditated regularly had much more stillness. We have so much stuff going on in our lives that anything that allows us some rest is surely a good thing.

In fact, science has shown that meditation has tons of health benefits, including helping to:

- reduce anxiety
- improve memory

- improve focus
- increase compassion and empathy
- increase creativity
- reduce stress

When I first started meditating, my technique was based on pure guesswork and an idea of what I thought meditating should look like, including calming music and slow breathing. I definitely performed a type of meditation, but I had no idea that there were specific techniques or different types of meditation out there. It took a man I was teaching to act to ask me what type of meditation I did to open my eyes, having been left mumbling 'just ... erm ... the closing your eyes and breathing slowly type.' I then went home to look further into what other people were doing, and here's what I found:

Spiritual meditation does what it says on the tin. Meditation originates largely from Eastern regions, where Buddhism, Hinduism and Taoism are the main religions. Spiritual meditation intertwines these religious beliefs into the practice, for instance it might include some chanting or talking about religious texts.

Movement meditation involves aligning our bodies and becoming more mindful of how we use them. This might be things like walking or doing yoga or martial arts such as t'ai chi.

Visualisation meditation is when you bring to mind images of things you want to focus on or something that makes you feel good. Think beautiful gardens and walks along the seafront.

Chanting meditation is fairly self-explanatory, and doesn't have to be religious in nature. The secular approach could be to come up with a mantra or affirmation that you chant out loud (*see* 'Affirmations' on p. 104).

Loving/kindness meditation involves focusing attention on someone else and sending them love as we breathe calmly and focus our attention towards compassion. The other person doesn't have to be aware you're doing this, and I use this mostly when I find someone disagreeable, to help me show up in a more compassionate way when I am around them.

Body scan meditation is probably my favourite to do with my online community and at my workshops. It's all about focusing our attention from head to toe on individual body parts and getting them to relax. We hold so much tension in our bodies these days that taking a moment to notice and change this is such a joyful way to check in with ourselves.

Breath awareness meditation is another of my favourite forms because our breath is so linked to how we feel. Try it for yourself. Take a few short, shallow breaths, high up in your chest. Within a few seconds, you'll notice that you feel a little more anxious than you did before. This is the power of our breath. To counteract this, we can perform breath awareness meditation where we become more conscious of our breath and take slow and mindful breaths, low down in our diaphragms. As you do this, notice the calming effect it has.

Then there is **zen** and **transcendental meditation**. These are different to each other, but both are much more intense forms of meditation. They are probably the types people think about when they hear celebrities talking about their 'practice' and, because I don't want to put you off, I'll let you google these after doing the basics first.

OK, so that was a lot to take in (maybe you can meditate on the stress of learning about meditation?).

Now a word of warning: when you first start trying to meditate your mind is going to have the attention span of a child who has just polished off a load of sugar and e-numbers. It's going to flag up everything you need to do and the memories you've been trying to avoid, and you're probably going to think, 'What the hell is this, where is my peaceful floating-in-bliss zone-out?' Meditation is a *practice*. At first, it might be much more challenging as you gently coax your thoughts back to your breath, your pulse or an object, but you will get there in time.

Years ago, I attended a yoga session during which someone talked about finding meditation challenging because her mind was so busy. In response, the teacher said: 'If in a 10-minute meditation you get 30 seconds of switch-off, then that's 30 seconds you didn't have before.'

Meditation has to fit into our lives and so I often practise what I have coined 'urban meditation'. This is the result of my recognition that my practice has to contend with the noise and bright lights of the big-city life and is rarely going to be done in silence or without challenge. Just yesterday, I meditated while my irritated daughter crawled under the chair I was sitting on and kicked her foot loudly on the radiator. I used this as a practice of patience and compassion, and believe me when I say it took all of my years of practice to focus my attention in a positive way.

OK, hit me with some meditation ideas

1 **Try out several types**. I gave you a whole list of types of meditation in this chapter, so play around, experiment and see what you find the most appealing. I switch up my styles all the time and my only aim is to give my brain that moment of switch-off, even if it really is just a single moment that day.

2 **Give guided meditation a go**. This is an easy way to start, simply because it's being guided by someone else's voice. There are tons of YouTube videos and access to free guided meditations online (in fact, here is a free meditation I recorded for you to get you started: iamhollymatthews.com/freemeditationforyou/). Please make sure you like the sound of the person's voice beforehand though or, like me last week, you might find yourself focusing on the person's mispronunciation of a word or poor grammar rather than the calm.

3 **Set aside a time**. Pick a time in your day and put it in your diary so you can try a 5-, 10- and then perhaps a 15-minute meditation. Committing to this regularly will hugely impact your happiness.

4 **Don't worry if you cry when you first start meditating**. It's common, as you sit with your thoughts, for emotional memories, worries or anxieties to come up for you. Be kind to yourself if this happens and know that you're not alone.

‹Meditation is brilliant, it just doesn't normally look anything like it does on Pinterest.›

#51

Let it go

You're lying in bed, struggling to get to sleep.
Perhaps you can hear a dog barking outside or the ticking of the clock
that you promised yourself you would swap for something less noisy.
You're desperately trying to get back to sleep but instead of your brain
helping by offering up soothing memories of your favourite moments,
you suddenly find yourself catapulted into an array of awkward,
regrettable and sad times in your life.

You find yourself running over past arguments and what you 'should'
have said, or pining for an outcome that you have zero control over.
Our brain loves to transport us back to our worst or most challenging
times because, essentially, we are desperate not to repeat them, and
ruminating over them helps us to feel somehow in control.

Telling people to 'let it go' is a pointless exercise. You're far more likely
to find them singing the track from *Frozen* than listening to your
advice. We can only ever really let go when we decide to face reality
and change our reaction to something. We have to be ready to do
this ourselves.

In my membership programme for The Happy Me Project, one of my
students asked how on earth she's supposed to let go of everything
that had happened to her. She stated that she didn't know how to
do it and, furthermore, that if she did let it go and walked forwards in
her life then she would have no 'excuse' for her lack of confidence. Her
fears and limiting beliefs all came from the experiences and trauma
she had gone through and holding tightly to them helped her explain
to the world why she was as she was. I explained that her experiences

were a reason for where she was, but they should never be an excuse for not doing the things she wanted to do. I also gently pointed out that only she could decide how she framed her pain. At some point, we have to decide if we want to hold tightly on to the pain and sit in a space of excuses, or fly high like Elsa and let it go.

We can't control what has been and grasping on to it only causes us pain. In the Buddhist religion, they often talk about 'attachment' being the root of all of our suffering. Nothing is permanent and so when we hang on to stuff (material possessions, relationships, feelings or objects), it's inevitable that we will eventually feel pain. This means that training ourselves in the art of letting go is going to serve us in our impermanent lives.

Who you are right now is made up of all the past experiences you have had. The knock-backs, break-ups, trauma, sadness and the loss, alongside all the funny, joyful, loving and beautiful moments you have experienced, too. So when you're lying in bed and your brain is forcing you to relive the painful memories, remember that the person you are right now is here *because* of all those moments and not in spite of them. If you've experienced pain, you've made mistakes or you have some regrets it doesn't mean you're broken, it means you're human.

In fact, and I'm going to get a little controversial here (because why the hell not?), how about we stop framing all our bad past experiences as 'the terrible thing that happened to me'. Maybe, as we explore in 'Change your BS story' on p. 128, instead of indulging in this victim thinking that keeps us in our pain, we take ownership for our part in things and at the very least how we have dealt with things that have stopped us from moving forwards. This is not about blaming ourselves but merely recognising that we need to stop letting our own and other people's past behaviour define who we are right now.

What is it that you won't let go of? What are the stories that you repeat on loop and won't let yourself move forwards from? Which of these old stories are still shaping your future, and not in a way that is beneficial to you?

I'm confident you just thought of something. Stay with that for a moment and let's remember one very important factor: your feelings are valid. Your raw and possibly painful emotions are allowed to be there. Start with giving yourself permission to feel. Give yourself a chance to say 'Do you know what? That thing that happened was awful and I'm angry about it. I feel so sad that this happened.' Allow space for this thinking, then once you really feel you've acknowledged this, start to move into a space of letting go and progressing.

If you find this difficult, ask yourself these questions: Why won't I let go? What is it that I think I will lose if I do? Could it be a sense of identity? Will I know who I am if I don't have this 'thing' hanging over me? Perhaps you pine angrily for your cheating ex because if you didn't then you'd have to face what you really feel, which is lonely. Or – like my student who was acknowledging what she went through in order to begin to let go – you might have to sit in the aftermath of the trauma and begin building up your confidence once more.

In short, we can honour the past and recognise what went on but also find the strength to move forwards (with all the learnings in our back pocket for when we need them).

I'm ready to get my Elsa on and let stuff go

1 **Make it essential**. What is your reason for letting go? What is not letting go making you lose out on? What are the benefits of letting go? For example, if you don't let go of the fact that you were bullied in high school, you may allow people to continue to treat you badly, have low self-esteem, not make new friends and stay trapped as a victim of something that is no longer happening. Recognising this can help you to see how essential it is to let this time in your life stay firmly in the past and release your grip on it.

2 **Be compassionate to yourself**. As you pick through the past, you might notice your own mistakes. It's very likely that there were moments when you took a wrong turn and made some bad decisions. Give yourself a break – who hasn't messed up now and then? Be gentle to yourself as you walk forwards.

3 **Let new stuff in**. Stop gawping at the past and focus on what new elements you'd like to bring in. 'Out with the old, in with new', as they say. Sometimes just the conscious decision to let go and let in is a very important starting point for us. Getting rid of the baggage of the past opens up a world of new possibilities.

4 **Sit in the aftermath with courage**. Once you've decided to allow yourself to let go and move forwards, you will find yourself pushed into feeling and noticing your current reality. This may be a little tough but stick with it.

'We can't control what has been and grasping on to it only causes us pain.'

#52

How to have
unshakable grit

In 2004, I had a night job at a local bank. I also worked in a museum cafe during the day with a red-headed American girl called Casey, who taught me how to make a fantastic cappuccino and steal the brownies without getting caught.

At this point in my life I'd been on TV and released a single, yet here I was once more, hustling to make money and on the side trying to crack some auditions.

At the bank, my job was to work out why people's mail had been returned, so I had to call the customers and say, 'Yo, you moved?' or something like that. Because I worked at night, there was never anyone else in the office with me, so I rarely called anyone or at the very least would call, let it ring once and then tick the box that said I couldn't get hold of them.

The reason I did this, apart from being hideously bored by the job, was that I could instead spend my time printing out my actor's headshots and CV. I would then send hundreds of letters to casting directors across the UK, and through doing this I managed to secure myself some meetings with casting directors and get some work. It was hard graft but I was relentless in my pursuit.

The acting world is full of people who want the job. The parts are few and far between and just getting your foot through the door requires a good agent and tenacity. I believe that the entertainment industry, with all its highs and lows, was my resilience bootcamp.

But what was it that powered me through all the 'nos' and the endless callbacks that led nowhere?

Why was it that I kept going?

Purpose.

When I first started learning about self-development I heard people talk about 'purpose' and I'm not sure I appreciated how lucky I was to have understood mine so young. I was about seven or eight when I decided I wanted to be an actress and from that day forwards there was nothing that would stand in my way. It was the fire in my belly and my constant, unshakable driver to keep going. It was my motivation to keep showing up and work two jobs, and it became the thing that helped to build my resilience.

Some people don't know what their purpose or 'why' is, yet understanding it is key when it comes to pushing through the tough times and keeping your head in the game.

Do you know what your purpose is? Have you ever considered it? Don't worry if you're staring blankly at this page with no idea, let's begin to explore some ideas.

Your purpose doesn't have to be anything really grand. There are lots of flashy purposes branded across Instagram, such as 'I want to help a million women become six-figure earners' or 'I want to build a school in a poverty-stricken part of Peru'. But it's OK if your purpose is that you wish to create a safe and loving home for yourself and your family. Your milder (yet equally valid and important) purpose might be that you want to bring more art and creativity into the world. Perhaps you're the funny friend and all you want from life is to look back and know you made people smile. These are not the obvious mission statements we might see on social media but they are as important to you and, ultimately, that's the point.

Resilience is described as the ability to bounce back from failures and recover quickly. Finding a reason or purpose makes being resilient far easier. Many descriptions of resilience talk about 'toughness', but I don't necessarily think resilience is about being 'tough'. You can be resilient and have tears streaming down your face and you can be resilient and sometimes not be 'OK'. Resilience is never about numbing your feelings and the British stiff upper lip mentality. Resilience is about not stopping. Happily, once you've found your purpose, keeping going becomes the natural next step.

'**Purpose is the life raft that keeps** you afloat until you get to the next good thing.'

Everyone can be resilient. The reason I know this is because I recognise that you've already been through some tough stuff in your life and yet here you are reading this book and dealing with the challenges life has chucked your way (well done on that, by the way!). So, if we all have resilience and it can be built up, how *do* we get more of it?

I want to roll with the punches, where shall I start?

1 **Create a 'mission statement'** or your 'reasons to power through' list. This could be made all pretty if you're a creative sort or just be a simple list. Refer to it when you want to give up, to remind yourself of your purpose and why the world needs you to keep going and try again.

2 **Recognise your resilience**. I think that resilience comes from looking at challenging times in the past. Consider what kept you going in these moments, was there any crossover in the things that you did? By doing this, you can discover clues and ways to cope. You may also find that your purpose was there all along (you just didn't have a name for it).

3 **Know your enemy**. Here are the enemies of resilience:

- perfectionism – getting stuck in the need to make parts of your life perfect
- catastrophising – exaggerating every incident
- the comfort zone – getting too comfy and not stretching yourself
- playing the victim/self-pity – thinking the world is against you

We will all slip into these habits at times in our lives, so zero judgement, but it's important to be mindful of noticing when you are and knowing how that impacts your resilience levels. For example, if you're stuck in your comfort zone, you allow no space for growth or failure – two things that will allow you to learn how to get back up. If you notice you fall into one of these categories, the first step is acknowledgement, and from there begin challenging the behaviours and learning to respond to life differently.

4 **Try and fail**. Trying lots of new things can help build your resilience. Give hula hooping a whirl, write a book, take up snowboarding or start an Etsy shop. Do things that stretch you a little. Push yourself to give it a go and see what adventures you can have. Every failure is just another step towards the next win and is also a sure sign that you are building your resilience (so in a roundabout way, you're still winning at something!).

5 **Be hopeful**. Hope could be dismissed as wishful thinking or a weak trait, but in fact it is crucial to keeping ourselves going forwards. The hope that things will get better, the hope that something good is on its way and the hope that you will fulfil your purpose. Purpose is the life raft that keeps you afloat until you get to the next good thing.

#53

Stop apologising for who you are

I am messy, chaotic, impulsive and stubborn.
In the past, I would have done anything to not have to admit this. All these labels come with judgement and imply things about my behaviour that may not be favourable. It would be easy to tell myself that who I am is not enough and to let a dark shame cloud engulf me.

I've learned to embrace my nature now, even if I do most definitely annoy myself from time to time. For example, I tend to rush into things too quickly in my eagerness to get started, which occasionally doesn't end well. Recently, I put a wall sticker up on my daughter's bedroom but was so excited about getting it up that I rushed and snapped it, meaning I had to buy a new one. I was like a kid at Christmas. I hadn't even taken my shoes or coat off before I was tearing open the box and chucking it on the wall. That, my friends, is impulsivity at its finest.

The benefit of this impulsivity, though, is that I am unafraid to press 'go' on things. If I have an idea then it'll very often be out in the world that afternoon and I'll work out the details afterwards. My first The Happy Me Project in-person workshop began with a moment of 'wouldn't it be lovely to get people together in real life and talk self-development', and then before I had time to overthink it the venue was booked and tickets were being sold.

So, what can we learn from this? It's clear that all of our seemingly negative traits can be positive in certain situations. You're messy? Maybe you're also creative. You're stubborn? Perhaps this means when you want something, you work hard and keep going until you get it. You're shy? Perhaps this also means you listen and are more sensitive to other's feelings.

We are all very nuanced individuals, a real mixed bag of personalities. There's space in this world for us all and yet many of us have a real issue with overapologising. I hear clients talk about being 'too much' for people and seemingly apologising for just being alive. One client filled in my pre-coaching questionnaire and I counted 10 'sorrys' in a two-page document. It was also littered with apologetic language, such as 'Does that make sense?' and 'I don't really know what I'm talking about but...' This might sound extreme but it's very common.

In many cultures, certainly my own British culture, saying 'sorry' like a tic is accepted as the norm.

'Sorry I didn't respond to your text message.' 'Sorry I missed your call.' 'Sorry, can I have your opinion on this?' We start sentences with 'sorry' on such a regular basis that many of us don't even realise we're doing it. In fact, I challenge you to listen over the next week and see how often you do it yourself (you can send me a message on Instagram @iamhollymatthews to let me know how high your count is).

You may be reading this and thinking, 'But it's polite to say sorry and I don't want to seem rude.' You won't sound rude! What you sound like (and I'm going to be unapologetic when I say this) is weak and a bit disingenuous. Are you really *that* sorry? It minimises the impact of the word when you are truly sorry if it's said every second word. What's more, it slowly begins to erode your confidence. Every time you overapologise you're telling your brain that your opinions and actions aren't good enough (and that's simply not true).

OK, let's look at what you should stop saying sorry for:

- **Making a request**. 'Sorry, can I get that coffee I've ordered' or 'Sorry, I know you're busy but can I grab that document please?' You're allowed to ask and you have nothing to say sorry for.
- **Taking time out**. Having a break, practising self-care and putting you first. You do not have to make excuses or apologise for this. A busy mum of four I know recently told me how guilty she felt that her husband 'caught her watching TV' (after she had done the school run and tidied the entire house) and I reminded her this was not something she should feel sorry about. Taking time out is imperative for you to function as a calm and rested human being.
- **Being excited about something**. Get me talking about people's minds and why we do what we do and I will carry on for three days solid. When you're passionate about your chosen topic and you find yourself getting chatty, don't apologise for this – most of the time it's very endearing.
- **Standing up for yourself**. If you've been wronged, or else someone is taking advantage or is perhaps portraying you in a light that isn't favourable, you're allowed to stand up for yourself (see 'Tell someone to 'eff off' on p. 96 for how to do this). A woman at one of my workshops once told me how a group of women at work had made fun of the way she speaks. In addition to feeling very angry about this on her behalf, I talked her through ways to confidently stand up for herself and not allow their snide remarks to make her slip into apologising for who she is.
- **Having an opinion**. I want to hear you loud and proud. If I don't agree then at least I will know I don't agree. Your opinion matters.
- **Choosing to walk away** from relationships that aren't serving you. Your life, your choice.
- **Having feelings**. Don't apologise for crying, for being angry, for being happy – you're allowed to feel.
- **Making decisions about your life** that those around you aren't keen on or don't understand. Sure, listen to the right people's thoughts now and then, and get some professional guidance where appropriate, but once you've made a choice then no sorry is needed.

You do not have to be sorry for being you, whatever that looks like. You are a whole wonderful mesh of quirks and eccentricities, so own them all and save the apologies for the important moments.

I'm ready to be 'sorry not sorry', where do I start?

1 **Tally up the sorrys**. Begin to notice when you apologise and how often, both in spoken and written form.

2 **Notice what triggers the sorry offloading**. Certain people and situations may spin you into sorry overdrive. Become aware, acknowledge and take steps towards changing this.

3 **Replace the sorrys with thank yous**. 'Thank you' can often reframe the sorry. 'Thank you for your patience' and 'Thank you for checking with me' can be used rather than 'Sorry for my delay' or 'Sorry for not getting back to you sooner.' This instantly feels more positive and keeps you looking strong and most definitely still polite.

4 **Pause before you speak**, especially when you're in your sorry-triggering arenas. Take a moment to consider your words carefully. *See* 'Watch your mouth' on p. 120 for more on this.

5 **Remember you'll always be too much for some people**. They aren't your people. Don't dumb down or dull your shine to accommodate others.

"You do not have to be sorry for being you, whatever that looks like."

#54

Treat yo' self

There are days when I realise I haven't stopped working or sat down for hours. I have tended to my kids (made their lunches and provided the 3000 snacks they appear to need every hour), and handled all the queries and demands from the people in my inbox. Without realising it, I have pushed my own needs (a soothing drink, a lunch break, a second to breathe!) way down to the bottom of the list. In these moments it's easy for me to go into 'soldier on' mode and forget that I'm important, too.

I know I'm not alone in this.

I know you too may have stopped looking out for yourself or prioritising your needs. When did you last treat yourself to something nice, such as 15 minutes of peace with your favourite book?

Treating myself in any form has always been a challenge for me. However, nothing highlights this more in my personal story than my former attitude to financial treats, which I'll share with you now.

I didn't come from a family with lots of money and as a child I was party to conversations about scarcity and lack. This worried me and I began to believe that if I didn't need something, then having it was greedy or excessive. Treating myself financially always felt like it came with a side order of guilt. So, for a long time, I rarely did.

As an actress most of my life, I found myself in a feast or famine lifestyle thanks to the contract-based nature of the industry. Even when money did come in, it made sense to save it. The idea of spending money on anything other than things that would feed back into my work felt wasteful.

It took me a long time to realise that treating myself financially was an 'issue' for me. You see as I have worked on my own self-development, I recognised that while I saw an innocence in saving, working hard and never allowing myself a reward, underlying all of those actions was a heap of limiting beliefs about my own worth that stemmed from my experiences in childhood.

I started earning money as a child (which people knew about) and I lived in an area where people didn't have lots of money, so it's not surprising that this brought up some 'stuff' for me. I realised I subconsciously developed the belief that 'if I make money, other people feel uncomfortable.' While this isn't a fact, I had the belief scurrying around in my subconscious, so my behaviour adapted accordingly, and followed me into adulthood.

This example is financial but of course treating ourselves is about much more than spending money. Treating yourself can mean cooking yourself your favourite meal or taking time to do your make-up. It could be the treat of a guilt-free day off or an afternoon nap. All of these experiences teach your subconscious that you are worthy of respect and are important.

So why do so many of us struggle to treat ourselves?

I don't think there is a person out there that doesn't have their own 'story' around treating themselves. Perhaps it's about feeling 'undeserving' or uncomfortable about nice things or experiences, or perhaps you feel a sense of shame about slowing down and relaxing when there's always more to do. Try to understand where these feelings may be coming from and remind yourself you *are* worthy of indulgence.

You may also struggle to treat yourself while others in the world have less time or resources than you – it might feel unfair. Let me get one thing straight: you not allowing yourself a day in your PJs to do some baking isn't going to impact those in poverty – the two things aren't linked. Have the PJ day and do some voluntary work; bake yourself a cake and give to food banks; they're separate points.

It's not selfish to treat yourself now and then. It's not selfish to want some time off or to occasionally want nice things. By never allowing yourself these privileges you are telling yourself that you are second best, that you don't deserve to enjoy these little pleasures, and it's simply not true.

When I know I have worked really hard on something, like the writing of this book, I will treat myself in some way. Now this might be as simple as sticking on my comfy clothes and ordering in an Indian takeaway or it could be that I treat myself to a nice long bath, with candles, and getting my hair done. There was a time when those things would have made me feel bad and I guarantee I'm not alone in that. I now see it as a form of self-respect and self-love. A little pat on the back.

Giving to others and caring for those around you is wonderful, and I'm pretty sure most of you reading this have no problem in this area. But remember, being kind to others is not mutually exclusive from being kind to yourself. I encourage you to cut yourself some slack once in a while and cheerlead and reward yourself, too – it'll make you happier.

I can't remember the last time I treated myself, where do I start?

1 **Explore the ways you might like to treat yourself**. Get ideas and write a list. Perhaps even create a 'Treat Yo' Self' wall chart or calendar with monthly, weekly or daily ways you can make treating yourself part of your life. If you need some inspiration, I asked my Instragram followers how they treat themselves and I've popped some of their suggestions on my website for you (some of them are genius!): www.iamhollymatthews.com/treatyoself.

2 **Give yourself the 'posh cups'**. Treat yourself the way you would treat your most prestigious guest. Get out the nice cutlery and fine bone china and let yourself enjoy those things too. We all have the stuff we only use on 'special occasions' or give to other people, but sometimes a special occasion is that you cleaned out the oven, which took two hours of scrubbing. (And 40 minutes of feeling guilty about how disgusting you had allowed it to get. I must add that I'm saying this because I just cleaned my oven and I feel like I deserve a medal.)

3 **Remind yourself that treating yourself does not mean you don't care** about those who have less. You can continue to help and treat others too, but just stop putting yourself so far down the list that you forget about yourself.

4 **Thank Bank**. Sometimes our treats do cost money and for those very special monetary treats how about starting your very own 'thank bank'. This is a little pot of money you put aside to reward yourself. This could be something you do weekly or as and when. It could be the old-fashioned coins-in-a-jar method, but whatever form it takes, it's your 'pot' to have fun. You may use it for the special occasions, the big 'wins' or just because you got through the month keeping your house fed and watered.

"Rewarding yourself is a form of self-respect and love."

#55

The real F word is 'forgiveness'

On 14 December 2012, Scarlett Lewis was devastated by the news that her beautiful child, six-year-old Jesse Lewis, had been murdered. Jesse lost his life along with 25 other people in the worst school shooting in US history, at Sandy Hook Elementary School.

Initially, Scarlett spoke of how her anger 'sapped all of her energy' and pain engulfed her. After a while, though, she decided that in order for her to move forwards she had to find forgiveness for those involved in the heinous event. Scarlett decided that anger and resentment would not be her story and she invited those around her to follow suit. She chose to publicly forgive the shooter and his mother, who had unwittingly armed him.

Reading her story for the first time, I did what many others probably did and thought, 'What the hell? How on earth has she been able to do this?' I remember thinking I'd want revenge and that I'd have to fight every human instinct to not attack back.

Scarlett Lewis had all those thoughts, too, and yet she chose to change the story. She recognised that there was nothing to be gained from hate and recrimination. As Mahatma Gandhi put it perfectly: 'An eye for an eye only ends up making the whole world blind.'

But forgiveness is hard, isn't it? On this level it seems *unbelievably* difficult, but even in our daily lives it can often feel hard to forgive.

Whether it's your partner for saying something awful in the heat of an argument or the friend who has let you down again, it's tricky to let go.

So why do it? What's the benefit of forgiveness? Well, let me tell you now, it's not about the other person. In fact, you don't even necessarily need to inform them of your forgiveness. When you choose not to forgive, you remain stuck in the past. You keep yourself squarely inside the story, and the festering resentment can eat you up. Forgiving someone is about you not carrying the pain and hatred around any more.

You can also forgive but no longer have the person in your life. Forgiveness doesn't have to come without boundaries, nor does it mean that you forget the lessons you have learned. Forgiveness simply means not giving the person or situation any more 'air time'. It means it's time to move forwards.

And it's not just other people we need to forgive. We need to forgive ourselves too, and that can often be harder still. We have stupidly high expectations of ourselves and when we mess up we are often way harsher on ourselves than anyone else would be.

Last year, my daughter Brooke was up for 'star of the week' at school. It was a huge accolade for her and I was incredibly proud. I'm lucky that I have created a life that means I can attend this kind of celebratory assembly and it was in my diary for 2.30 p.m.

At 2.45 p.m., I was listening to a podcast and folding some laundry when a wave of dread washed over me. I was late. I grabbed my keys, mumbling 'no, no, no' to myself and raced to the car. I hurtled through the school gates and into the hall to see Brooke's angry and let-down face, which broke my heart. I had missed her moment.

I held back the tears (kind of) and tried to apologise as she brushed me off and shoved me away. When you're the parent of a child who has lost their other parent for whatever reason, the pressure to be at everything is immense, and what was truly gutting was that there was no real reason for my absence.

I was so critical of myself. At first I didn't want to forgive myself and instead fixated on how my actions were probably going to give her lifelong issues and trauma. However, I knew this way of thinking wasn't going to help, so instead I took her and her sister to TGI Fridays and showered Brooke with cake and balloons. I apologised, I showed her my sadness and disappointment, and I gushed about how proud I was (I went so overboard that Brooke told me to do it again, because she wants more balloons).

Forgive yourself for the mistakes you make. You're human and none of us can avoid them all the time. Having compassion for yourself can also help you to recognise the imperfections we all have, and perhaps help you to develop a more forgiving nature towards others.

I want to forgive, where do I start?

1 **See things from another person's point of view**. For example, the person who burgled your home might be struggling with addiction, with no support network. Or the cheating spouse might be deeply lonely and seeking affection elsewhere. A good exercise is to write three letters discussing what happened. First, your letter (easy, probably full of fury and anger); second, a letter from the point of view of the person who wronged you (much harder, you have to walk around in their shoes and understand their motivation and the context of what they did); and finally a letter from a 'third party' (an impartial person looking at both sides and giving their interpretation of what happened).

2 **Understand the difference between 'actions' and who a person is**. Separate the two things. What you or someone

does isn't who they are, it's what they did. As I wrote this, my eldest daughter burst into the room and threw some tea towels on top of me in a fit of temper, after being asked to do some school work. Does this mean she is a mean tea towel-throwing devil child? No. It means she is struggling to manage her emotions today and did something I am sure I will receive an apology for in the next hour.

3 **Gift yourself the present of letting go** and living a better life. Affirm your forgiveness out loud, to yourself, to the person or to a friend. Forgiveness is the courage to let go of the anger. You will reap the reward of joy and a lightness that will take you to a more positive place in your life.

4 **Write a letter to yourself**. In this letter, you will pick the thing you want to offer forgiveness to yourself for and write a compassionate letter of understanding.

'Forgiveness is the key to changing your story.'

#56

Your house is a bloomin' mess

Do not look under my stairs!

Do not open the door to my shed or glance behind my sofa. Why?
Because there you will find the chaos that is often my life, shoved
into boxes and hidden from view. Is this relatable? Don't feel bad
if it is.

My brain springs from one thought to the next like a drunk kangaroo
and often I leave a sea of destruction in my wake. Drawers and
cupboards left open, the clothes I took off chucked on to the bed and
scribbled notes strewn on tables.

If I didn't care how I looked or felt then this carnage wouldn't matter
to me, but I do care, and very quickly I begin to feel bogged down by
the clutter. I also heap all kinds of judgement on myself about why
keeping my house in order doesn't come naturally to me.

The clutter we see in our homes often contributes to the clutter
we find in our minds, and so it makes sense that mess might make
us feel overwhelmed, anxious and stressed. The mess causes the
stress by distracting our minds, filling us with guilt and shame (I
know I'm not the only one who does a 'shame tidy' before guests
arrive) and reminding us that 'our work is never done'. All of this
mentally drains our batteries. What's more, it's also damn annoying

if you can't find what you're looking for because it never really had a place to start with.

To counteract my slovenly tendancies, I recently slipped on to the Mrs Hinch side of Instagram. For those who aren't familiar with Mrs Hinch, she is a blogger who became famous for her cleaning tutorials and amazingly well-kept home. She has written books on cleaning hacks and has created a fabulous community of (mostly) women who have beautiful, shiny homes. I found myself scrolling though the #Hincharmy hashtag thinking, 'Where is all their stuff?' and 'How do they get their kids to play ball?' It is a brilliant approach, but I had to be honest with myself and admit that it just wouldn't work for me.

The reality for most of us lies somewhere in the middle between the houses of the 'Hinch Army' and 'Slobby Susan', but the benefits of decluttering your home should not be underestimated. Clutter is often stuff we no longer need but hold on to anyway. The old clothes that we promise ourselves we are going to 'get back into', the keepsakes from past relationships or jobs, or items that we promise ourselves we are definitely going to sell on eBay (is this just me?). When we get rid of this stuff we are also letting go of the emotional baggage related to the physical things and allowing ourselves to move forwards.

I moved house soon after my husband died. We had always intended to do this and had bought a new place together. The house was having renovations done on it, so a lot of my possession were put into storage, particularly the 'kitchen stuff'. In the period before my new kitchen was ready, I had the bare minimum of kitchen essentials and washed as I went.

When the kitchen was finished and my two big boxes of 'kitchen stuff' came back to me, I opened the box with a sense of slight despair. I had done without this stuff for so long that I realised the majority of it wasn't needed. I decided to be ruthless and ask myself some hard questions. Do I need and want this? Will I ever use this? This was made harder by the fact that my husband Ross was the 'chef' in our home and was very particular about the quality of stuff we had. Getting rid of kitchen items he would have used (but in reality, I wouldn't) felt like a betrayal and was more emotional than I had imagined. It was also, though, a relief to see only half a box actually come back into my home and the rest rehoused via charity shops.

It's time to clear your place and get some headspace

1 **Take it one step at a time**. When it comes to decluttering, don't try to tackle every room or hidey hole at once. Pick a place and pick a time and get to work bit by bit. For every item, ask yourself: 'Do I use it, need it, love it or want it?' Be really honest with yourself.

2 **Crank up the tunes**. Make the tidy-up and declutter work fun and speedy. I hate tidying up but I know that the end result makes me feel brilliant. My solution is this: do a 10-minute tidy-up or speed clean with your favourite music blaring and dance moves chucked in for good measure. This way, you may even encourage others to get involved. (It's the one way I can get my kids to tackle their chaos.)

3 **Make a checklist**. Oh, I know, it's nerdy, but I have a nightly checklist to help me keep on top of house work, chores and organisation. I'm not going to sit here all holier than thou professing to always complete my checklist, but it definitely keeps me on track more than it doesn't.

4 Think about how it makes you feel when everything is in its place. You can see surfaces and you know that if at any moment a visitor were to appear unannounced (which is ridiculous and should never happen!), you would feel calm and relaxed. This calming feeling of your tidy home is going to help you to switch off and enjoy the lovely space you have created for yourself to live in.

"The clutter we see in our homes often contributes to the clutter we find in our minds."

#57

The worst has happened

A few times in our life something really tragic or traumatic will happen. A time when life deals you a blow that punches you in the gut and sometimes literally makes you drop to the floor.

Mine came in February 2014 when I was sitting in a hospital bay with my husband, Ross, and his mum, Dionne. Ross had been brought in via ambulance with a terrible headache and sickness. We had been in the hospital all day as he was poked, prodded and checked over. There had been no sense of urgency and I had the feeling we were about to be sent home with a packet of paracetamol and told to follow up with the GP.

It was late at night, we were tired and wanting to get home to our daughters, Brooke and Texas, when the hospital bay curtain opened and two doctors stepped in.

'I'm sorry, Mr Blair, but we've found an egg-sized tumour in your brain. We will do what we can – chemotherapy, radiotherapy, surgery – but if there is nothing more we can do, we will just keep you comfortable.'

I felt the news wash over me and the air was sucked from my body. My head went fuzzy as my brain tried to process what had been said. Then, as the reality engulfed me, I reached my hand out to the bed to steady myself.

'Tumour.'

'Brain cancer.'

'Brain surgery.'

Words that would terrify the strongest among us were suddenly thrust into our reality.

From that moment on, my life changed. In 2017, Ross eventually did die from that awful cancer, and my family's world was kicked to a place we didn't ask for it to be.

It still feels unbelievable to think about Ross not being here and grief is certainly a process, one I live with every day. But even early on in my journey I understood that when we are forced to deal with the BIG life stuff, we have a major choice: we can decide to let it break us or we can decide to let it make us.

None of us are immune to the tough stuff, even those people who you think have breezed through life. And the truth is you won't really appreciate your moments of joy until you've felt pain – how annoying and messed up is that?

To give an example, let's consider childbirth, which is something many of us experience. When I was pregnant for the first time with my daughter Brooke, I tried, as most expectant mothers do, to imagine what childbirth might be like. Basing my knowledge of labour on what I had watched on various TV hospital dramas, I was under the impression that I was going to experience constant, agonising pain.

The reality of giving birth, though, for the most part, is that we go through phases of pain. We have a painful contraction, followed by a moment of respite. Another painful contraction and then a moment to catch our breath. Our lives work in much the same way.

Something tough happens to us – a job loss or a break-up perhaps – and then we have a moment in which to recover. Then along comes another challenge (or contraction) – maybe the death of a loved one or a failure – and then another period of calm.

In order to lead a happy and fulfilling life, we have to recognise when we are in a lull or period of respite. Sometimes they're short, so we have to be alert and quick to recognise them to ensure we pack these in-between moments full of life, love, good experiences and appreciation.

Ross's death was one hell of a contraction that I didn't ask for, just like you didn't ask for whatever tough times you're experiencing. As you're reading this, you might be desperate to stop whatever's happening, but I imagine it's out of your control and so I'm asking you to stop grasping and to pause a moment.

Take a breath, have a cry, feel your shock, feel your fear, and then get ready to dig deeper than you ever have dug in your entire life. I'm willing you to decide that you are going to do whatever it takes to get you through this next difficult stage in your life and to decide that you are going to be happy between the contractions, regardless of what is going down. Maybe that's a divorce, an argument with your best friend or the fact that the kids have just left home. Whatever it is, look for the joy between the periods of pain.

This won't always be easy, but deciding to do it is the first step.

I believe in dealing with life head-on and that when the tough stuff happens there can be a sense of clarity that cuts through the unimportant crap and lets you sift out what really matters to you. These times can be defining, draw-a-line-in-the-sand type of moments that can propel you into being brave or taking bold action in your life, if you allow them to.

You didn't choose what's happening, but fighting the inevitable is going to prolong the pain. Remember that the contractions don't last forever and we always get to decide how we show up in these moments. So roll up your sleeves and prepare to get yourself through to the next stage. A new version of you will emerge in this new phase of your life, and you decide who that's going to be.

What to do right now

1 **Connect**. You are not alone, my friend. The awful crap connects us all deeply and when you reach out to people they will share their own fears and their own loss and you will see that we are not so different.

2 **Remember the contraction theory** and that nothing stays the same. Know that this will one day feel less painful (even if this feels like a completely useless nugget of information right now).

3 **Commit to taking things one step at a time** and being kind to yourself. Hell, you've (possibly) not had to deal with this before, of course you're going to feel chaotic and lost, it would be weird if you didn't. Looking too far ahead when you're in the middle of the tough stuff isn't going to help, so just walk through this next 'thing', until you realise you've travelled quite a way.

4 **Ask for help and accept help**. I know this can be hard, I still find this hard to do, but remember that people want to help and sometimes they really don't know how. Give them stuff to do (this could be a great time to get some free meals and your washing done – every cloud, people!). For more on this, check out 'Ask for help' on p. 124.

5 **Focus on what you *can* control and not what you cannot**. What can you do today that you are totally in control of. Can you get dressed? Can you go for a walk? Can you catch up with a friend? Can you have a self-care day where you binge-watch your favourite TV show in your pants and eat copious amounts of ice cream? (Some days, this is exactly what's needed!) If I had focused on trying to

stop my husband dying of cancer, when we had no more options, it wouldn't have stopped him dying and it would merely have made the process more painful. Put your energy into what you can control.

6 **Remind yourself that you are strong** and you are capable. This is true even when you are shaking with fear about what the next steps will be, even when you have tears running down your face and you haven't washed in a week. Inside you, you have everything you need to get through this stage in your life. I believe in you!

‹**Life cannot break me for** I know how strong I am.›

#58

Music to my ears

'You've got to search for the hero inside yourself, until you find the key to your life' Heather Small sang loudly through my ghetto blaster. It was 1994 and 10-year-old me listened to those lyrics intently, soaking up the message in Heather's velvety smooth voice and then rewinding my tape and starting again.

Music has always been a huge part of my life. Growing up with parents who were punks and loved music clearly had an effect on me. There was always music in our home, and I would sing for hours and hours, practising and recording myself. I even started a band with my sister Beki and our neighbours, and we were constantly putting on 'shows' to anyone who would watch (or anyone who was forced to watch).

At every point in my life there has been a track that defines the era and I have no doubt that you too will have your own soundtrack. Some of the songs will be emotive and sad and some will be uplifting and take you back to times of joy and excitement. This could be extremely useful in my profession as an actress: I could tap into my 'sense memory' to help me create the emotions I needed for a given scene, and so I had a playlist of 'sad songs' that would help bring me the tears when required.

Clearly, then, music and emotion go hand in hand. This is backed up by science. In 2019, a study found that music therapy was consistently associated with a reduction in anxiety and stress in critically ill patients. I mean, I'm sure you have your own anecdotal evidence that listening to calming music impacts your mood or levels of anxiety but it's always nice to hear there is real science behind what we intuitively know.

Music is also said to improve our performance, our endurance and our memories. Plus music therapy has been shown to aid recovery in those suffering from depression. All in all, music is just brilliant at shifting our moods.

What's more, it can help us learn. As I sit here writing this chapter, my youngest daughter Texas is bellowing out her times tables to music. Music has been shown to help us retain basic facts and aid our memory skills, and I have first-hand experience of this. Before learning her times tables in this way, Texas struggled to retain the knowledge, yet as soon as it was fun and musical, she got it.

Tony Robbins, a motivational speaker, talks frequently about getting into 'peak state'. This is when you're most alert and at the height of your performance levels. If you have ever witnessed a Tony Robbins event you'll know he is often on stage for 10 hours a day and yet his energy is simply incredible. He achieves this elevated level by getting himself fired up and into his peak state before shows. He has shared openly that he uses music to do this and believes that not only can music impact your own personal mood, but it also affects how you interact with others.

Think about the power of music to motivate you when exercising. Listening to Eminem's 'Lose Yourself' as I drag my sorry self round my neighbourhood for a run is the only thing that distracts me enough to keep going, and I bet you have your own power track for similar moments. When a boxer is stepping into a ring, they have a track that pumps them up and gets them into the right frame of mind to win. This isn't an accident, this is because music really does have that level of power over us, and I want us to tap into how you can make use of music to enhance your mood and life.

Turn up the base and let's get to work

1 **Power playlist**. Create a playlist of music that gets you motivated, and pick your 'going into the ring' track – mine is 'Warriors' by Imagine Dragon. (If you need inspiration, check out The Happy Me Project Spotify playlist.) Then use your playlist to start your day, get you motivated when you have something important to do, or for when you need to be your strongest self. I'd love to hear about your favourite power songs when you've chosen them. Message me on Instagram @iamhollymatthews or Twitter @hollymatthews and I might even pop your songs onto The Happy Me Project playlist.

2 **Solo karaoke**. This isn't about being the best singer or performing for anyone else (unless you want to). This is about having fun, connecting with yourself and the music. Search YouTube for your favourite musical artists, type 'karaoke' after their name and you'll find tons of playlists of songs to sing along to. I love doing this and can often get lost in the moment. Sometimes I look up and whole hours have gone by as I've done an entire Mariah Carey set and am knee deep in Christina Aguilera's *Stripped* album. Have fun and let yourself go.

3 **Join a choir**. Hold up! I know you might think I've lost my mind, but there's been a resurgence of choir singing and it's no longer as linked to religion as it once was. The websites www.van.org in the USA and www.bigbigsing.org/find-me-a-choir in the UK will give you tons of options. The benefits of a collective sing-along have been shown to help improve our sense of connection and community, as well as being really good fun. If nothing else, it will be a great story.

4 **Escape to somewhere else**. Music is an instant way to teleport to another world. Pop on your headphones, close your eyes and soak up the notes that soothe and calm. Create your 'escape and unwind' playlist to help you relax. My daughters have a 'bedtime playlist' and when that music goes on, it certainly makes me feel sleepy.

‹**Music is brilliant for** shifting our mood.›

#59

Night-time ritual

A good night-time routine and a good night's sleep are the key to a productive day. If I have spent the evening organising my clothes for the day ahead and prepping what I will need to do, I can then rest easy into a calm night's sleep and awake feeling energised and prepared.

Going from awake to asleep for some of you may be as easy as turning off a light, but many of us need to be lightly coaxed into our sleepy slumber. Either way, creating rituals that help this process along is really worth the effort.

I am a night owl by nature. Some of my best ideas come late in the night. This means that if I'm not careful I can start trying to put together a launch strategy for my latest business idea as the clock strikes midnight, when I should be sound asleep in my bed.

To counteract this behaviour I have to find ways to wind down and make my evening a slow 'dimming' of my day rather than a 'lights off and get to sleep!'

Just as for morning routines, there are some proven formulas and ideas about what a 'good' bedtime routine might look like. However, as in 'Morning ritual' on p. 80, I am not going to profess that I have the 'secret sauce' to evening harmony. I will, however, give you some ideas to chew over so that you can piece together a routine that is going to work for you and your circumstances.

A quick note to any new parents or parents of young children: the idealistic stuff we will chat about in this chapter may make you want to scream out 'Why won't this child just sleep!' This is perfectly understandable. I ask you to read this chapter only so you can gain an understanding of the influence of your night-time routine, and encourage you to seek out the gems that might help, but always be kind to yourself. I understand that sometimes it is simply impossible to do this stuff while you have other unpredictable little humans to factor in.

So, let's look at some ideas for your night-time ritual. You can use my **prep**, **pause** and **ponder** system to help work out your own plan. This means focusing on the prep, 'How can I prepare ahead of time for tomorrow?'; the pause, 'How can I allow my mind to switch off?'; and the ponder, 'How was the day I just had and how would I like tomorrow to look?'

Let's start with the **prep**. This might mean getting tomorrow's outfit ready, perhaps laying out your sports clothes and the breakfast dishes, and sorting out anything your kids may need. Take away choices and potential stressors from the you of tomorrow and allow 'night-time you' to rest easy.

It might also mean getting out your pen and paper, whiteboard, planner or to-do lists, and getting ahead of your tomorrow in this way too. Often, our inability to wind down comes from having too much going on in our heads. When we plan out our next day we can allow our brain to trust that we are on track and know what we are doing. For more ideas on this, *see* 'Be more boring' on p. 144.

Now it's time to find your **pause**. What rules will support you being able to switch off? I'd love to climb high on a 'positive mindset pedestal' here and pontificate about how my evenings are a 'no phone zone' and social media-free sanctuary, but it would be BS. I have my phone nearby and I chat to my friends and even allow myself some scroll time.

I do, however, know that too much of either too late into the night will affect my 'dimming down', so I have created some rules. For instance, I have a 10 p.m. cut-off from social media and work, and I put timers on my apps to force my hand with this. Other people might suggest rules about not working from your bedroom, removing all devices and no caffeine after dinner.

Does your bedroom support your pause time? When my husband Ross was here he would often laugh at me when I said we needed to create a bedroom that was a sanctuary or boudoir, but I stand by this notion. If your room is cluttered or distracting, it's going to leave you thinking about the mess or the peeling paint that you've been meaning to get sorted but haven't. It's not about a 'bedroom make-over' necessarily, but at the very least get into your bed and notice what is drawing your attention in a negative way, and then correct it. Think about what the last thing you see will be as you nod off and the first thing you'll see as you wake.

Use your senses to help you pause. Can you create a gorgeous 'bedtime smell' (I know people love lavender, but you can use whatever scent is your favourite) or perhaps use a soft, snuggly blanket (weighted blankets can be brilliant if you need some extra help). Or perhaps try a bedtime playlist of zen-like music.

The final step is your **ponder** time. Think about ways to end the day on a positive note. No day will ever be perfect, but at the end of each day it is lovely to end on a high (even a mini one). To this end, every night as I put my kids to bed I ask them: 'What are your three favourite things from today?' If it's been a tough day then this process might be harder but it's then that it becomes even more important. I do exactly the same for myself, and I often also ask myself: 'What are my daily wins?' or 'What have I learned today?' This may be something you chat about with someone else, think about quietly to yourself or, for extra points, write down in a journal to look back on at the end of the year.

Ponder time might also be taking time to visualise. As you close your eyes, imagine a time in your future when you're doing something you really want to be doing – perhaps a job you want or a lifestyle you'd love – and let yourself walk around in this 'vision life'. See through your eyes, feel what you feel, hear what you hear and play in this 'future history' as you fall asleep. Over time, this will begin to programme your subconscious to understand that this version of your life is a possibility.

This might seem a little heavy in terms of the structure, but investing the time in yourself like this will have huge pay-offs and set you up for success tomorrow.

Time to dim the lights and find your routine

1 **Create your routine.** Think about what we have discussed and choose some elements to add to your evening routine. Remember the three Ps: prep (for the day ahead); pause (on jobs, phone chat and work); and ponder (about your daily wins, what was brilliant about your day and what you have learned).

2 **Create your environment.** Perhaps it's time to move things around a little in your room, to get rid of distraction and give life to a tranquil bedtime space. As a person who really hates tidying but is really affected by clutter, I recently saw something referred to as '17 things'. This means just picking up and tidying 17 items in one sitting (mine is before I sleep). You choose the number 17 because it doesn't seem as many as 20 but actually it has a huge impact on how a room looks.

3 **Note your triggers.** What is going to keep you awake? Become aware of these things and find ways to lessen their impact by finishing earlier or not doing them at all. If you know you'll binge-watch a crime drama if you start, then maybe bedtime isn't the time to begin a new series. If you know that looking at your phone will spiral you into two hours of scroll time, maybe put your phone on charge in another room and walk away.

> **'The key to a great day is the** prep the night before.'

#60

What if it were all taken?

Picture the scene. You're sitting in your home, it's dark and the rain is pelting down outside. Your washing basket is full, the dishes wait accusingly by the sink and you can hear your children having a row about Roblox in the next room. In that moment, it's easy to feel despondent and frustrated by life, to slip into a juicy little 'pity party' and text your friend to moan (misery loves company, right?).

This is all perfectly natural, I'm with you, and occasionally it's fine. If, however, the 'pity party' turns into a month-long 'pity parade' and you suddenly lose all perspective, then we are going to need to rein it in.

I never like to turn sadness into a competition of who's had it worse. I don't like it because it's pointless. Pain is pain, how we experience everything is individual, and the fact that people are starving in India doesn't negate the fact that you feel sad that your dog Noodle died last week.

That being said, sometimes we need to take a moment to get some perspective and to reignite some appreciation for our lives. This is that moment.

Let me get you to take a step back and give yourself a chance to take stock. Use your imagination and begin to guide your mind around your current reality. Hold up. I know your brain just went straight to the 'crappy bits' of your life, so now let's lovingly escort it back to the bigger picture and examine every part of your life.

This includes the people you love. Think about those friends and loved ones for a moment now. The wonderful memories you have of them, the laughter you've shared and that time when they did that thing that you promised you'd never tell a single soul about. Allow your mind to wander back into them with ease. The holidays you've shared, the nights out and the countless meals. Reminisce about the 'firsts' you've had together, the moment when you met, the experiences you've delighted in, and let yourself be immersed in these lovely memories.

Now bring yourself into the present moment and think about what you have. Picture your home. What's your favourite room or hang-out space? Maybe you spent a lot of time decorating somewhere or have a picture of something or someone you love up on the wall. Do you have a seat that's yours? My Grandad David always had a seat that was 'his' and a drawer full of sweets (if you were lucky, you might be offered one). Mentally relish thinking about all the little nooks and crannies of your home that you love and have created.

Take time now to think about your workplace or business. What are your favourite parts of this? Do you love to chat with Debs at work about her ditzy gaffes over the weekend and her newest beau? Do you enjoy the thrill of learning and the excitement of being part of a team?

Do you have children or pets that bring joy to your life? Catapult yourself into some of your most special moments with them and savour the fond memories you have.

Consider the bigger picture, the country you live in or your neighbourhood, and what that offers you. Even the roughest places usually have joy, spirit and heart. How about your lovely neighbours and the postie who makes everyone smile with his cheerful whistling?

Take it all in and embrace the daily wonders.

Are you smiling yet? As I write these words and review my own life, I am smiling (in fact, my daughter just saw me and asked me why I was smiling at my laptop).

Now imagine what would happen if you were to wake tomorrow and it had all gone. No family, no friends, no home, no food in the fridge, your health has deteriorated and the world is bleak. What would happen if the work dried up, the postman lost his glee and your comfy seat broke?

Would you then appreciate what once was? Would you pine for the home full of washing and the bickering family who made you laugh at their antics? Would you crave the safety of the community you know so well and the body that helped you live fully?

It's too easy to moan and complain and focus on the frustrations of daily life (read all about it in 'Stop moaning!' on p. 24), but this brings us nothing but heartache in the long term. Let this be your wake-up call. This is your moment to soak up pleasures that are all around us.

I totally get this, but it's hard, how can I stay on track?

1 **Practice makes perfect**. If you have been in a loop of complaining, being ungrateful and just generally being an unappreciative buffoon, remember that it's all about practice and retraining your brain to focus on the joy, not the 'lack of'.

2 **Say thank you more often**. To the postie, the nice waitress in the local coffee shop, your mum and dad and your siblings. Thank your children and the supportive spouse. Make 'thank you' part of your life.

3 **Deflated to elated**. Feel the frustrated, angry feelings of being fed up, notice the rage bubbling and get comfortable with observing the ebb and flow of this. We can't escape these feelings but we can get better at sitting with them and flowing through them. As they rear up, sit for five minutes and take stock of what's going on for you. Question why you might be feeling as you are and how you might see the situation differently. It might even be useful to get up, move, splash your face with cold water or jump up and down on the spot, to literally 'change' your state. Know that these feelings are not 'forever feelings' and choose appreciation instead.

‘Notice the important things and people in your life, bank them in your mind and soak up every moment.’

Letter to you

Hooray, you made it to the end of my book, or perhaps you dipped in and out, or went straight to the end. However you got here, you're here now and I'm down for it.

I don't know whether you bought this book because you're miles down the road of your self-development journey and this is another piece to that jigsaw or if this is your first ever self-development book (how exciting, I feel extra lucky if this is the case). Perhaps you're a member of my family and/or friendship circle and I forced you to go out and buy it. However you're here, I'm glad that you are.

This book is something I'd wanted to write for a long time and I honestly had no clue how to go about it. Like pretty much everything I have ever done though, I jumped in with the idea and worked out the route as I went along. From the outset, however, I knew how I wanted it to feel and I knew I wanted it to be easy for you as the reader to digest.

Now that you're part of my community or my gang (or whatever word doesn't make you cringe – I nearly wrote 'posse' but realised instantly that I couldn't pull it off), you will be able to tap into all the other resources I give out on my social media platforms, much of it for free.

I want you to recognise that reading this is just the beginning. Personal growth and understanding who you are at each stage of your life are constant processes. Even though I do all of the things that I have taught you in this book, I remain a messy, imperfect student of keeping my own mind happy.

I hope that if you take anything from this book it's that there is always an opportunity to change the BS story that is holding you back. That we can always start afresh and decide that we want to go down a new route and be a different version of ourselves.

There will be some days when things are hard and some days when you slide back into old behaviours that you thought you'd banished for good. Let's leave the judgement and the shame in the bin where they belong and lean into who we are at our core.

While reading this book, you may have recognised that there are areas where you need professional help and I encourage you to seek this. There is never one route to us feeling happy and we are such nuanced and individual people it's likely we need a whole mix of different ingredients to help with that. Often, we also need different things at different points in our lives.

Roll with it all, try different things, be brave and know that while 'knowledge is power' you don't always have to find ways to 'fix' yourself, because you're not broken, you're human.

Now I want to get to know you. I want to see your highlighted light-bulb moments, your YouTube videos on the lessons you've learned from this book and your blogs sharing your journey. Tag me on social media and share photos of you with your book far and wide. I adore seeing who I have managed to reach and will try to always respond to your messages. We are always stronger together.

I firmly believe that a movement, maybe even a revolution, is taking place in the self-development space. That may sound a little grand, but I just mean that we've all become tired of not being taught how to navigate our own minds. We're tired of the clashing, disorganised and frustrating experiences we live through, and more and more people are seeking ways to help themselves. Now is our time to say, 'Enough! I want to feel happy more often than I don't, and it's down to me to make this happen.' Trust me, you can. I do it, my clients do it and now it's your turn.

Life is just a series of choices. Do I go this way or do I go that way? Our lives rarely turn out how we thought they would, do they? But man, life is short and we have to live our lives in a way that makes us happy. My best choices have required bravery and staying in my own lane and I don't regret any of them (even the ones that felt hard to make at first!).

So, wherever you are in your life, make yourself happy first. Obviously, don't seek to hurt others, but also remember that you can't live your life solely for other people either.

Seek out happiness, love and moments of joy and ride the waves of the crappy bits of life. Start now, get up, shake it off and do something today that will get you even a tiny bit closer to the next happy moment.

Check out my website www.iamhollymatthews.com for more resources and come and say hi on social media. If you do post anything, remember to tag #TheHappyMeProject because I want to see your journey and cheer you on as you go.

I believe in you and, even if right now you don't believe in yourself, you can borrow my belief in you until you get there (which you will).

Holly x

Acknowledgements

My mum, Clare, my dad, Brian, and my incredible sister, Beki. I wouldn't be anywhere without you guys. I love you completely.

My extended and totally amazing family – The Wilkinsons, Osbournes, Blairs and Goughs – you're the best. Special shout-out to Dionne, Rob, Matty, Ashley and Xanthe for having the girls while I wrote this book, and my Aunty Denise for all her support and love.

Thanks to Junie Poonie, Mantra Jewellery and my incredible photographer friend Kayleigh Pope (for always taking the best photographs of me and joining me on random escapades).

To my wonderful friends for putting up with me never texting back and ghosting all WhatsApp groups.

Thank you to the team at Awesomesauce Marketing for setting me on the right track and helping me make sense of my chaos. To Jen at Fuzzy Flamingo for helping me put my initial proposal together, which helped me get this book out in the world. BBC CWR for letting me chat to the listeners every week and to Channel Mum for their incredible support in the most difficult times. To Sapna my VA, a total superhero who has made my life easier, my wonderful clients and The Happy Me Project community, I appreciate you all so much.

A huge thank you to my wonderful editor Holly for her excellent name and making this the most lovely and supportive process, while always being honest with me. To Bloomsbury and all of the team who made this book a reality – what a bunch of total legends.

And finally to Brooke and Texas for being the most resilient, awesome girls in the whole world and for (sometimes) allowing me the peace and quiet to actually write this book.

Other resources

Remember you're not alone. There are other people who have walked the same path as you, and there are supportive communities ready and waiting to help you through your journey.

I believe there is nearly always more than one route to feeling good and getting support, so please find below my list of several amazing organisations doing important work that you might find useful.

The Samaritans
Call the free hotline at any time, from any phone: 116 123
https://www.samaritans.org

Mind
www.mind.org.uk

Grief Encounter (supporting bereaved children and young people)
www.griefencounter.org.uk

The Brain Tumour Charity
www.thebraintumourcharity.org.uk

Widowed and Young
www.widowedandyoung.org.uk

The Happy Me Project Membership
If you'd like to continue your journey with me, my no-nonsense life coaching membership is ready and waiting to scoop you up and give you a safe space to land.
www.iamhollymatthews.com/happymeprojectmembership

The UK Council for Psychotherapy website can be a useful place to begin if you're looking for a therapist: www.psychotherapy.org.uk